Compulsory Dancing

Compulsory Dancing

Talks and Essays
on the spiritual
and evolutionary necessity
of emotional surrender
to the Life-Principle

by
Da Free John

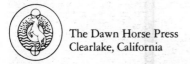

The Dawn Horse Press
Clearlake, California

First published under the title *Conversion*, September 1979
First revised edition published April 1980
Reprinted February 1983, August 1984
Printed in the United States of America
International Standard Book Number: paper 0-913922-50-1
Library of Congress Catalog Card Number: 80-80912

Produced by The Johannine Daist Communion in cooperation with The Dawn Horse Press

Contents

About Master Da Free John

The Adept Da Free John was born Franklin Albert Jones on the third of November 1939. Until his second or third year, he lived in a world of sheer light and joy—"the Bright"—where he knew no separation from others. He was born, out of an Enlightened Adept's free Choice and Compassion, with the specific Purpose of Instructing spiritually sensitive people of today in the "Way of Life." In order to fulfill this sublime Mission, he had to sacrifice his conscious Oneness with the Transcendental Reality prior to his birth. Even the extraordinary condition of the Bright was necessarily surrendered to allow the individual Franklin Jones to pass through the process of physical, emotional, and mental growth. However, his original Impulse to Guide others to the Realization of the Transcendental Being or Consciousness never ceased to inform his life, which from the beginning was destined for greatness.

Throughout his childhood, the condition of the Bright that he had enjoyed as a baby would reassert itself in the form of uncommon psychic and mystical experiences, as well as physical symptoms such as sudden attacks of fever or skin rashes with no diagnosable medical cause. These signs of an active kundalini (or Life-Current) gradually subsided in his eighth year and did not return until he reached the age of seventeen.

It was in 1960, after a "crisis of despair" with the world he lived in, that the spiritual process spontaneously resumed its transforming activity in full force, blessing him with the experience of "a total revolution of energy and awareness," which yielded two crucial insights. First, he realized that in the absence of all seeking and problem-consciousness, there is only the one Reality or Transcendental Consciousness. Second, he understood that this Reality or Consciousness is Man's true Identity and that all else is only a super-imposition of the un-Enlightened mind.

Equipped with these twin insights, Franklin Jones began to immerse himself in a conscious spiritual discipline of acute self-inspection. For almost two years (1962–1964) he sequestered himself, intensely observing the dynamics of the separative self-sense, or ego. This phase was punctuated with numerous psychic experiences, one of which led him into the company of the American-born teacher "Rudi" (Swami Rudra-nanda), who instructed him in a form of Indian kundalini yoga.

Early in 1967, while studying at the Lutheran seminary he had entered at Rudi's behest, Franklin Jones underwent a "death" experience, restoring him temporarily to the Bliss of Transcendental Being-Consciousness. Again, he emerged with an important insight: that his whole search had been founded on the "avoidance of relationship," on the recoil from Reality in all its countless forms. As his inner attitude to life changed, he also recognized the limitations of Rudi's yoga—a recognition that, in 1968, prompted him to seek out Rudi's own teacher, the late Swami Muk-tananda. During his brief stay at this renowned yogi's hermitage in India, he had his first adult experience of total absorption in the Transcendental Consciousness. Swami Muktananda acknowledged this unique yogic achievement in a written document, confirming that Franklin Jones had attained "yogic liberation." But, intuiting that the "formless ecstasy" (nirvikalpa samadhi) that he had enjoyed for a moment did not represent the highest form of Realization, Franklin Jones continued to submit himself to the wisdom of the spiritual process that had guided him throughout his life.

His intuition was confirmed on September 10, 1970, when he entered the permanent Condition of Sahaj Samadhi, which is coessential with the Transcendental Being-Consciousness itself. He had "recovered" the Identity that, though never really lost, he had surrendered in order to effect his human birth. Soon after his God-Realization, the Adept was moved to Teach others and Transmit to them the Condition of "the Heart," or the All-Pervading Reality in which everything inheres. But those who came to him in the early days were ill-prepared for his Teaching and Transmission. After nearly three years of "almost muscular" struggle with his students, which weakened his physical body though not his Energy and commitment to their Enlightenment, he undertook a pilgrimage to India.

He not only wanted to clarify his Teaching Work but also purify his relationship to those who, like Swami Muktananda, had been helpful catalysts in his spontaneously unfolding spiritual discipline. It was during that period that he changed his name to "Bubba Free John"—"Bubba" denoting "brother" (his childhood nickname) and "Free John" being a rendering of "Franklin Jones."

Upon his return to America, he began to Teach differently, involving his devotees in an experiment of intense experiencing of both worldly "pleasures" and so-called "spiritual" joys. He gave them the opportunity within the growing community to pursue all their obsessions about money, food, sexuality, and power, as well as conventional religiosity and mystical states. Every single "Teaching demonstration," however abandoned or unconventional, had the sole purpose of showing devotees the futility of all seeking and all types of experience, and that only understanding availed.

Out of this "Teaching theatre" grew not only a profound insight on his part into human psychology, in all its different forms of manifestation, but also a new, more formal Teaching approach. In November 1976, "Bubba" Free John ceased to have frequent intimate contact with his many devotees. In the following three years he lived in relative seclusion, creating much of the "source literature" that now serves the community of practitioners as one of the empowered Agencies of his Teaching.

In the fall of 1979, the Adept dropped the name "Bubba" for the spiritual address "Da," meaning "Giver." Having endowed the community of devotees with all the necessary means for their spiritual maturation, Master Da Free John is now in the "hermitage" phase of his Work where, together with mature practitioners, he lives the simple existence of a free renunciate. His retirement from active Teaching Work and from institutional involvement of any kind is not a mere withdrawal from the body of devotees. On the contrary, his seclusion allows him to concentrate on his real Purpose: to Transmit the Transcendental Condition, unencumbered by any external obligations, and thereby to quicken the spiritual maturation of all practitioners in the different stages of practice, as well as to extend his benign Influence to ever-wider circles of people.

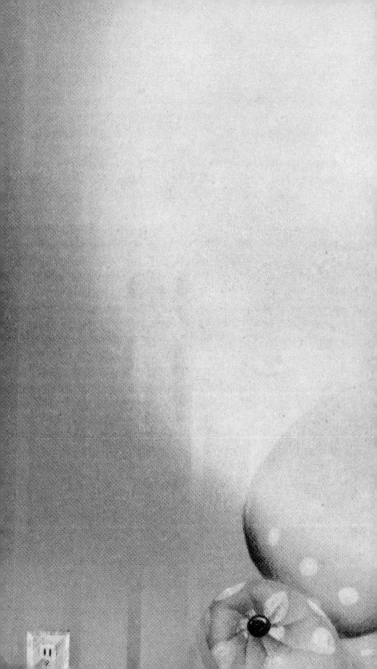

Are You Willing to Be Happy?

by Saniel Bonder

The Truth that is God and Life is sufficient in and of Itself. We are not truly separate from That. We are happy only in ecstatic or self-released Communion with That. To release the entire body-mind into Communion with the Radiant and Unknowable Divine Reality is happiness. It is not that the act of such release produces effects in us that are happiness. Rather, the sacrifice, or Communion itself, is happiness.

Da Free John
The Enlightenment of the Whole Body

Are You Willing to Be Happy?

Everyone is always <u>seeking</u> to be happy. This book is about <u>being</u> happy, about recognizing the true nature of happiness and being <u>willing</u> to be happy in every moment — now, and now, and now.

Da Free John teaches that the realization of happiness depends upon the emotional conversion of the human heart <u>from</u> Narcissism, or self-possession, <u>to</u> Divine Communion, or love of God. Our ordinary self-centered life is expressed emotionally in cycles of fear, sorrow, anger, guilt, doubt, lust, and anxiety about "me" and "my" pleasures and "my" death. We can instead enjoy the disposition of love, trust, and self-yielding service in all relations, self-forgetting sympathy with all beings, intuitive bodily certainty of Eternal Life, and radiantly happy faith in God. The way of this great conversion is first to recognize that our own lives and the entire world are arising in each instant within the Spirit or Being that is God, and then to surrender, with profound feeling and with every breath, into that Living Transcendental Being.

No matter what else Da Free John may speak about — and the range and depth of his considerations are astonishing — he has always principally spoken to this one event, the emotional and spiritual conversion of our hearts. And all his play with devotees during the early years of his Teaching Work was dedicated to this transition, which requires a profound reversal of the energy of the being from self-possession to ecstatic or self-forgetting love of God.

The popular religious message today is full of stories about experiences that make people believe in one or another Deity and that magically transform their lives. While true emotional conversion may be associated with an incident or series of incidents in one's experience, it does not depend on any experience. It converts one not to believe in God, but to direct, unmediated Communion with and dependence upon God for one's very life. Emotional conversion involves intuitive Awakening by Grace, through "hearing" or understanding the Divine Teaching to the point that you spontaneously "see" or feel the living, Radiant Energy of the universe, the "Vision of God." It simply becomes obvious that no matter what you think or feel or do, God is the Condition of this and every moment, and God is presently living you.

However, you must literally choose to live on the basis of this Enlightened revelation. You always have the option to turn back upon yourself—thus, you must choose in every moment to live and breathe and speak and act from the point of view of one who is alive in the Spirit of God. In the following talks you hear Da Free John asking again and again: Why do you insist upon living as if God were not present and obvious? Having felt the Divine Presence of Love, why should you ever again contract into fear and self-possession? To choose to live as a converted, Enlightened personality is the great leap of faith, the great act of surrender to and dependence upon Grace. This gesture must be repeated afresh in every instant with and as the whole body and mind until the reflexes of fear and all other reactive emotions disappear entirely from the being. Make no mistake; it is difficult. But at a certain point you find you have no real option but to choose God and to will to be happy in every moment.

The "climax" of these considerations, then, will be your own emotional conversion. Are you willing to live with Freedom and Wisdom in the Vision of God? 9 Are you willing to cease believing your neurotic mind and to begin to presume the Enlightenment of your heart and whole being? Are you willing to become a saint in your disposition and action, a force of radiant, healing ecstasy in the human world? Are you willing— now, and now, and now—to be happy?

Saniel Bonder
The Mountain of Attention
Middletown, Calif.

Note to the Reader:

These talks were mostly conducted in small gatherings of devotees with whom Da Free John has worked closely and personally for years. He addresses, however, self-centered emotional, sexual, and mental habits that are universal. This became dramatically evident when we used these discussions as the basis for intensive seminars with other members and friends of The Johannine Daist Communion. The considerations catalyzed great positive changes in the moral, religious, and marital lives of hundreds of people. Thus, we feel that this book will serve in any interested reader the intense self-examination and change of heart that are the core of true religious awakening and practice.

The Great Principle of Life-Practice

An Essay

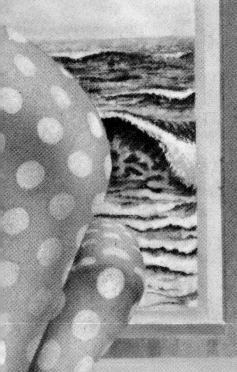

We are each inherently obliged to fulfill the Law in human form—to be Love. Love, or the spiritual and Transcendental Realization and Incarnation of God, comes into expression on Earth only through Man, or else it does not appear at all. It is through Man that the higher potential of Earth can be Realized and Shown. Therefore, do not aspire to what is merely active in the Realm of Nature. Do not aspire to the level of creatures and elemental processes. Do not aspire to the mediocrity and subhumanity of the usual man. Rather, be Inspired and Instructed by the Spiritual Master, the True Man. Be Inspired to Incarnate Love, Ecstasy, Divine Communion, Radiant Life, and all the Excellence of Man in God. Transcend yourself in God-Love, and fulfill the Man by Sacrifice, or constant Ecstasy.

Da Free John
The Enlightenment of the Whole Body

The Great Principle of Life-Practice

An essay by Da Free John

T he usual Man is Narcissus, the self-possessed, the eternal adolescent. He is contracted upon himself at the heart. His willfulness is automatic, unconscious, bereft of the feeling-intelligence. Therefore, he is weak-willed, unable to transcend himself through continuous growth, higher adaptation, and Ecstasy, or Enlightened self-surrender.

The usual Man is a problem. He is self-divided. All his alternatives contradict one another. He is always at war with the parts of his own experience. He is contracted upon the various functions of his own body-mind. He is in shock, suddenly existing as himself alone, unable to discover the Truth of his own Origin, Help, and Condition.

The problem of the usual Man is emotional dissociation. The body-mind or psycho-physical being that is the usual Man is automatically tending to contract upon itself, to be differentiated from all experiential phenomena, to possess and fill its emptiness with the objects of all experience, to protect itself with all knowledge, to separate itself from the mysterious emotional demand of all relations and events.

The strategy of the usual Man is the avoidance of relationship, the avoidance of free emotional association with all beings and events. Each function of the human body-mind is tending toward emotional dissociation from experience. And the root-effort in all forms of psycho-physical dissociation is emotional and total psycho-physical contraction from the All-Pervading Life-Principle, the Living Being that is the Truth and Transcendental Condition of the body-mind and the world itself.

14

The usual Man is mysteriously committed to self-possessed emotional dissociation from the Universal Life-Energy, and, therefore, from all experience—since all experiences, events, relations, and beings are arising as spontaneous manifestations or modifications of the Universal Life-Energy, the Radiance or Light that is the Matrix and Destiny of all forms of appearance and "matter." The heart of the usual Man, or the emotional-psychic root-being of the unawakened individual, is chronically disturbed, contracted upon itself, dissociated from the Universal Life-Principle that is its own Condition, Help, and Origin. Therefore, the body-mind or total psycho-physical being that expresses the heart of the usual Man is chronically disturbed, contracted upon itself, dissociated from all experience, all phenomena, all events, all relations, all beings, and even from the fulfillment of its own functional existence.

The Salvation or Happiness of Man is in emotional conversion, or the conversion of the heart from the automaticities of self-possession to the conscious Realization of Ecstasy, or self-transcending Love-Communion with the Universal Principle or Being that is Life. Such emotional conversion is awakened through constant study and hearing of the Teaching of Truth and constant seeing or intuiting of the Living Divine

Presence in the Company of the God-Realized Man and the Community of devotees of the Living God.

Our fundamental responsibility is literal and deep psychic Love of the Presence of Life. We must surrender to Life in order to be full of Life. The Life-Current is the "Holy Spirit," the Divine Effulgence or Grace whereby we may be Transfigured and made One with the Living and Eternal Divine Reality. But we may be thus Transformed only if we transcend all emotional contraction upon the self and, instead, Radiate as Love of the Life-Principle or Living Person that is God. It is emotional conversion to Life that heals our dis-ease. And one who is thus converted will naturally extend his enjoyment of freely-circulating Life into disciplines that prevent toxemia and degenerative abuse of the structural body-mind.

Right emotional submission to the Life-Principle in every moment permits transcendence of enervating emotional and general psycho-physical contractions. And right emotional submission to the Life-Principle in every moment is the basic form of spiritual or religious practice. It is Ecstasy, or Radiant release and transcendence of the self-contraction or ego-obsession that separates us from Life, or the Grace and Person and Condition of the Living God.

PART I

Emotional Surrender to God

Talks to devotees

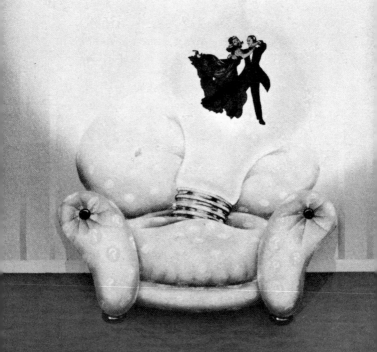

We must surrender to and into the Present God. God is not elsewhere in relation to us now. God is always Present, Alive as all beings, Manifest as the total world. Our obligation is not to invert and go elsewhere to God, nor to extrovert and exploit ourselves in the self-possessed or anti-ecstatic mood that presumes God to be absent or non-existent. Our obligation is to Awaken beyond our selves, beyond the phenomena of body and mind, into That in which body and mind inhere. When we are thus Awakened, our lives become the Incarnation Ritual of Man, whereby only God is evident and only God is the Process of the present and the future. That Way of Life is not bound to this world or any other world, nor to any form of attention in body or mind. Rather, the Way of Life is Ecstatic, God-Made, Free, Radiant, and always already Happy.

Da Free John
Scientific Proof of the Existence of God
Will Soon Be Announced by the White House!

The Only Cure of the Loveless Heart

D A FREE JOHN: The practice of heartfelt devotion to God in relationship to the Spiritual Master is the true and perfect Way of life. It is the only path that realizes the fundamental understanding that, after all your searching comes to an end and even during the entire effort of your seeking, and even now in your most profound meditation, you are emotionally turned away from the event of existence. You are never in any moment emotionally satisfied. In order to be free of this negative, reactive disposition, you must realize what this gesture of emotional dissociation is altogether. You must become responsible as the heart, or the emotional, feeling core of your being. Everything else follows from this practice, and everything that is necessary for your existence and your spiritual practice will thus be revealed to you by Grace.

I have already described to you how the process unravels, and I could continue to describe all kinds of practices that become natural and useful in moments here and there in the process and that you will at some point simply assume as a functional discipline — but fundamentally there is one practice, one basic discipline. Contrary to common presumptions about religious and spiritual life, that practice is not to seek for God. The fundamental practice is to confront and transcend this emotional dissociation right now, and in every present moment. It is to surrender to God as the One Living Personality, the Companion of one's heart, and to allow that condition of surrender to be the

Condition of one's life. Thus, one is no longer Life-negative or heart-negative, but one persists in love moment to moment, and is ecstatic.

In order to be happy, you must know that you have complete freedom to love and to be ecstatic in every moment. Yet your whole life has been an emotional refusal of all experience, of God, of relationship, of the Radiance of your existence. You have been contracted upon yourself with emotional force, and no amount of thinking, considering, experiencing, desiring, exploiting, and manipulating yourself in the world can affect that contraction. No awakening of the kundalini[1] touches it. It has nothing to do with the kundalini. You can have kundalini experiences until you are yawning with boredom, yet you will not have touched this emotional recoil at all.

You tend to think of yourself in terms of your limitations — your thinking, emotional reactions, bodily sensations, and desires. You pursue your religious life as well as your ordinary life while thinking of yourself as an actor or a person defined by those limitations. You have little certainty about anything beyond

---

1. The kundalini or kundalini-shakti is the "serpent power" of esoteric spirituality. It is the very Creative Power of the universes. Traditionally, it is said to lie dormant in man, coiled at the base of the spine. It may be awakened spontaneously in the yogic practitioner, after which it ascends within him, producing all the various forms of yogic and mystical experience. Da Free John indicates that this internal spiritual force is eternally awake, but that Man is not awake. Therefore, he recommends no efforts to awaken this force itself, but puts all attention to our awakening to the prior, eternal, and always present Nature and Condition. In the course of such spiritual practice, internal force may be awakened as a secondary event, but it is regarded and dealt with in quite a different manner than is recommended by the yogis.

your thinking consciousness. You feel physical desiring with great certainty, but the idea that there is a Consciousness that influences you or that is fundamental to you is relatively alien, or at best occasional. You think about God, and you feel that some day you will make up your mind about whether or not there is a God, but what do you think you will do differently then? Look at the people who claim to have found God—they do not seem to have changed very much. They were depressed, now they seem gleeful. But are they Enlightened, God-Conscious, moral, compassionate, wise, sane, fearless, and spontaneously happy at all times?

You must enter into a presumed association with God as the intimate, heartfelt Associate or Companion of your life. The creation of relationship with God certainly is a great gesture. It is the only cure of the loveless heart and of the whole life of suffering. In the process, you become quite open to natural association with dimensions of existence that you have not previously taken into account. You begin to recognize that apart from your frantic, self-possessed consciousness, in which the mind is not released to God and the brain is not relaxed in the Life-Current—apart from this obsessive, thinking pattern of mind that you typically dramatize, there is a greater dimension of mind that does not engage in the thought process. Perhaps you also suddenly realize thoughts and intuitions for which you previously have had no sensitivity.

When you begin to presume an association with God, observations of the world have new significance for you. Perhaps you were not noticing previously, or perhaps now new and very remarkable things simply do begin to happen. Now you are trying very hard to acquire a dimension of mind and knowledge, even literal practical knowledge, from or with the thinking mind itself. If you can relax your thinking mind into the higher mind, which is prior to thought, higher psychic intuitions and even information will appear in your patterns of thought. A higher understanding will come into consciousness.

You will also notice then that your life is changing, by virtue of this same heartfelt Divine Association. Just as you observe changes in your consciousness or mind, in which new dimensions appear spontaneously and intuitively, you also notice that your vital, physical life, your ordinary life of desiring, is beginning to change too. You become much more effective, more capable of choosing to do something and actually doing it. Many positive, remarkable, and interesting things begin to happen to you.

Thus, the heart is the primal center of consideration. Everything that is body and mind is the emanation of the Divine, which we identify via the heart principle, or Life-positive emotion, Radiance, love, prior to contraction, self-possession, and fear. The effects of the gesture of the heart must appear in your mind and body. The body-mind must be Transfigured by love, by emotional self-transcendence. Nothing less than this emotional practice is true or sufficient. We are willing to do all kinds of things—even to go into long periods of seclusion and to deprive ourselves of bodily comforts and pleasures—just to experience extraordinary effects in mind and life. We will engage in all kinds of practices, you see, that are self-manipulative. Some of those practices are creative in an ordinary sense, but they are not this practice of the heart.

You have not committed yourself to the practice of love, or emotional association with God and all existence. You are still committed to emotional dissociation. Emotional dissociation is Narcissus, self-possession, the ego. If you would transcend the ego, you must deal with the emotional gesture of the being from moment to moment. Transcendence or dissolution of the ego is entirely an emotional matter. Thus, there is no transcendence of the ego until love appears, until there is self-transcendence via emotional sacrifice of the body-mind to God, the Living Personality, the All-Pervading Life-Current, Who is expressed as everything and Who absolutely transcends everything. You must choose this sacrifice, this loving gesture. If you will choose it, if you will make this emotional commitment, then all experience becomes Divine Revelation to the point of ecstasy and transcendence of everything in God.

You must "see" God truly. Then you must enter into right association with the Spiritual Master and into right practice in his Company. The mere sighting, the mere association with the body-mind of the Spiritual Master, even any form of Remembrance and association with the Spiritual Master, is God-Contemplation. Practice association with me in the truest spiritual sense, awakened in your understanding that this body-mind is a "Murti" or Image of the All-Pervading Principle, alive and conscious. If you simply enter into ecstatic association with me, you will always stand in a temple with me where ecstatic speech is understood, where we are all whirling and can speak only the Truth.

The ecstatic relationship to me is the key to practice. Do this heart-practice in relation to me with heartfelt attention, and use me as the Form, or Sacred Image, through Whom to enter into Communion with the Personality of God. In this way God-Communion can be realized very simply. All the elaborations of spiritual life follow from this natural devotion, which ultimately includes all of mind and all the Mysteries of existence.

The Fire of Transformation

DA FREE JOHN: Devotees who enter this Church are literally entering a fire, the fire of the Presence of God. If they are just mediocre, immature people, unprepared for esoteric practice, they can sit with me in the meditation hall and engage nominal practice of the esoteric disciplines, and they will have some experience or understanding as a result, but that understanding will not have the same profound quality as the understanding of the genuine Adept, because the immature individual cannot tolerate the fieriness. He or she will waste it and dissociate from it, particularly in an emotional way. If you tend to dissociate emotionally from the Spiritual Power, from the Life-Presence of the Spiritual Master, from the Divine Presence, then you also prevent the spiritual process from manifesting in your own life.

As long as you have emotional problems and are fitted to the conventional mind, you cannot realize any more of the spiritual process than the ups and downs of feeling disturbed and feeling consoled. You must come to the point in your practice where the Presence of the Spiritual Master, the Living Presence of God, is completely obvious to you, even bodily, moment to moment, so that you can actually feel it working in the body-mind. Likewise, you must have a capacity for surrender to that Force, so that it can continue to purify the body-mind at every level. Whenever it meets some obstruction, some tightness, some stress, some tension, some mental obsession, it will just work on that obstruction for years and years and years and years creating a difficult life for you. As soon as the obstruction dissolves, suddenly that area of the body-mind feels full. Therefore, you are smart to become a devotee first. Then the process need not be made difficult by virtue of your own resistance. Much of what is difficult about the process is simply your resistance, the fixations of mind, the emotional reactivity, the conventional street mentality, and the physical habits that create toxic, enervated, negative bodily states.

The higher and spiritual physics of the evolutionary process in which we are involved is the conversion of the body into energy and the conversion of energy into consciousness. Most people who approach me generally are only considering the idea of the transformation of the body into energy, and such consideration does not develop to a high degree except in rare cases. To go beyond the mere development of energy in the nervous system, therefore, to the realization of the Transcendental Reality, true Consciousness, the Infinitely Radiant Being, is an extremely rare event, for obvious reasons. The mechanical life that people develop through action-reaction in the Realm of Nature creates obstructions that do not easily disappear. You see how difficult it is for you to move beyond the most rudimentary psychological and emotional problems. What must you do in order to be translated into absolute energy and consciousness? Bodily Translation into Light requires a great leap, an extreme of practice, and you must be fit for it. You must let many things go. You must let everything go finally, and allow that letting go to be the end of it.

But you keep returning to your problems. Your commitments last a few hours and then you forget all about them. You cannot fulfill this process while your loveless tendencies are still possessing you. Thus, you must practice with a will, from the heart. The heart is the key to the practice of real or spiritual life. People tend to focus on the dimensions of the mind or the body, and to lose the focus of the heart. Nevertheless, the principle of spirituality is at the heart, and the fire of the spiritual process is awakened there. That fire is not situated at the perineum, nor is it up at the crown. It is at the heart, at the place of Infinity, the root of the being, the feeling core of the body-mind.

Therefore, if you are constantly struggling with emotional problems, the spiritual process cannot be effective in your case. Only a rudimentary religious association is possible in a life that is characterized principally by emotional phasing. Transcending the phases of emotional dissociation is a requisite for entering into the truly esoteric or higher development of this Way. Thus it was that traditionally the esoteric initiation was available only to those who had passed through a period of apprenticeship. The Adepts did not go downtown and initiate ordinary people into the kundalini process or reveal esoteric techniques for exercising the higher aspects of the nervous system in meditation. Spiritual initiation is not meant for people with emotional problems, and therefore it should not be given to such people. Such people need not be turned away, but they must be integrated with the culture of Truth. They must take up the Way of Life in its fullest terms at every level for which they personally can be responsi-

ble. When they represent a psycho-physical
mechanism that can hold the Divine Light and Force,
then the esoteric process of the higher stages of life will
begin for them.[1]

Surrender is the mechanism of transformation,
heartfelt surrender to God, and the great Mechanism in
Nature that quickens the surrender of human beings is
a human individual who can act as Spiritual Master, an
individual who is transparent to the Life of God and
who can enter into relations with devotees. The Life-
Presence that is the Spiritual Master and the Divine is
granted to the devotee through his or her relationship
to the Living Spiritual Master. The gift of Grace is
monitored constantly by the quality of heartfelt practice, or heartfelt surrender. If you spend your life using
the Spiritual Master for conventional purposes, wasting
your life and the Divine Force he brings to you with
endless vulgar emotional problems, then that conflict
is also all you will realize. Your practice does not become the great spiritual process if you associate casually
with the Spiritual Master. The spiritual traditions are
filled with endless stories of people who were intimate
with enlightened men, even the intimate personal ser-
vants of enlightened men, yet who gained nothing because they were not rightly related to the Master. In
spite of their proximity, they approached the Master
through conventional forms of relationship, while, by
contrast, people who had practically no outward inti-

1. Da Free John has described the life of the human individual, from
birth to full spiritual maturity, in terms of seven stages. For a complete
discussion of these stages please see *The Enlightenment of the Whole Body* and
The Eating Gorilla Comes in Peace, by Da Free John.

macy with the Spiritual Master frequently became the greatest examples of the devotee in his Company.

If you do not "see" the Spiritual Master, if you are not, through heartfelt sympathy with him, awakened to his true Condition, you cannot practice rightly in his Company. You must realize that the Spiritual Master is a Spirit-Presence, not merely a collection of flesh and bone. If this truth is not clear to you, then you cannot practice rightly. You waste your life failing to fulfill the law of devotion. If you have not "heard" the Teaching, if the Truth is not awakened in your own insight and understanding, you cannot "see" the Spiritual Master. You must "see" the Spiritual Master, and you must "hear" this argument. You must appreciate what the Spiritual Master is so that you can surrender to him in Truth.

The Devotee Increases the Delight of God

30 **D**A FREE JOHN: There is a danger in mere verbal consideration of the Teaching — reading, thinking, and discussing the Teaching and the Way of Life. You can become profoundly consoled by the verbal consideration alone and think that you are actually practicing the Way. Yes, you may enjoy a certain level of understanding, but true self-transcending practice is another matter. Therefore, the verbal consideration should be finite and to the point. It should orient you to the real and necessary event, the conversion of the body-mind to love through feeling.

Sin is simply emotional dissociation. Narcissus is emotional dissociation. What you are suffering is only emotional dissociation from experience and from all relationships in every moment. There is a density, a contraction, a recoil recognizable in feeling and in the body. It is primarily associated with the heart, but it emanates to every aspect of the body-mind. It is at the root of all the strategies of your life. That recoil is emotional dissociation.

There are reflexes that operate in all the areas of our functional life. When we shock one of these reflexes, the experience is so profound that the natural mechanism recoils into a chronic state or pattern of reactivity. This reaction is not a temporary solution, such as the physical recoil from something very hot. Emotional reflexes become frozen, fixed in place through shock. Many such reflexes are effective in the complex of your body-mind, and they reveal themselves in various ways. The fear of death, for instance, should illustrate to you how profound your fundamental emotional reaction is and how firmly it is fixed in your born existence. You have emotionally recoiled from the fact of death and, thereby, from Life altogether. The quality of emotional dissociation is always present in all of your experience. There is a way, however, to transcend this reaction. You can enter into self-transcending Communion with the Living Principle and Reality of Life and be liberated thereby from all illusions founded on recoil from love.

People talk about sin constantly, but the solutions they offer do not bring sinning to an end. Sin is emotional separation, emotional dissociation in this moment, and therefore separation from God, self-possession, betrayal of others, collapse from love, from happiness, from blissfulness. Sin is "missing the mark" with the body altogether. When you feel as if the point of Truth is in your heart, as if Truth is to be discovered within the heart, you are just feeling the cramp in yourself. What is to be discovered is not within you. You are collapsed from Radiance, from love. Even bliss is not sufficient Realization. You think of bliss and associate it with God, but bliss is merely profound pleasurableness. It is not in itself necessarily associated with the ecstasy of God-Love. You can enter into the blissful self-root of the body and the heart, but absorption in the bliss awakened in this manner is not sufficient for God-Realization. You can become profoundly blissful without being changed emotionally. While blissful, you will still feel this fundamental, self-possessed emotional dissociation from events, from existence itself, from God. Bliss must become ecstasy. When bliss becomes ecstasy, then it is love. In other words, when bliss transcends the self, it becomes love. And love is the Principle of existence.

Therefore, everything is superficial except this emotional consideration. You must be able to continue with it in every moment. Not merely as a thinking affair — you must constantly be able to bring your attention into the feeling domain so that you do not mightily collapse from it. And you must learn the artfulness of the good heart that is awakened through this consideration. Such artfulness includes all the matters of devotional service, sacramental action, and esoteric meditation.

You may be familiar with the conventionally dualistic, religious approach to devotion or service to God or the Spiritual Master. In that approach you basically empty yourself and do not have a blissful, bodily association, a love association, with God. You are not ecstatic. In the conventional mind, living for God has a negative connotation, suggesting grayness and dryness. But the service I am considering is bodily worship or ecstasy, wherein you are oriented without concern to God, to the Infinite. The true devotee acts to increase the delight of God. All of manifest existence is already the pleasure of Infinity, but through bodily, sacramental service, through surrender to Infinity, you enhance and participate in that pleasure naturally. If such sacramental action is performed properly and in the right spirit, in fact if any service is performed in the right spirit, such service is bodily worship. It is bodily bliss. And beyond bodily bliss there exist bodily Transfigura-

tion, Ecstasy, and Translation into the Divine Domain
or Transcendence of all bodily and mental states.

The Wizard of Oz

DA FREE JOHN: People enact a kind of ritual when they become involved in so-called serious consideration of this Teaching and Way of Life. First they talk together about profound matters and confess many things about themselves that were previously hidden. Then someone in the group summarizes what is the proper attitude toward the subject, based on a real understanding of life in Truth, and at that point the people in the group—having already completed the ritual of talking very profoundly and relieving themselves of secrets they had never told before—begin to speak as if they have now understood and assumed this practice profoundly, once and for all. Then, at the next several meetings, the group presumes that it need not pass again through that ritual purge. Rather, they ritually play out a positive feeling about the discussion of the last meeting. That superficially positive attitude tends to become the dominant quality of their lives until the next time they must engage in a great purgative ritual or a "serious" consideration.

People who indulge this pattern do not tend to pass through the real emotional change that I have been discussing with you. Rather, they only indulge the ritual itself, at the end of which everybody talks and acts as if he or she were really practicing now. Perhaps a few real changes do occur here and there, mostly at a cultural level. But for the most part such changes are only superficial, external to the heart of true change. Thus, rituals with fixed liturgies or scripts typically become established in the culture of this community of practitioners. These ceremonies are just as fixed as the rites that are repeated week after week in downtown churches. You use the principle of "let's pretend" to bless one another. Having performed the ritual of seriously dealing with one another, you then accept one another's false confession and false or merely pleasant face. You may act more pleasant than usual, but you have not passed through the real change. Nevertheless, your act of being relatively pleasant and assured, as if you have finally understood, is accepted by your fellows as if it were the real change of the heart.

In the film *The Wizard of Oz*, three characters come to the Wizard to acquire something they lack—a mind, a heart, and vital strength in the world. Even though the Wizard turns out to be something of a sham, he gives them each a gift that, in the feeling of the story, seems to be genuine. The scarecrow, for instance, has no brain. So the Wizard says to him, "The only thing you lack that all other people who have a brain do not lack is a diploma." Then the Wizard gives the scarecrow a diploma. But the scarecrow has not developed his intelligence. He has never passed through the process of adaptation to the functions of the mind. All he has done is to receive a diploma. The diploma is sheer nonsense, a lie that he now feels or imagines is a truth about himself. In the story, however, everyone now accepts him as if he were no longer lacking a brain.

Very superficial changes are the focus of this story, but the same superficial orientation to personal change tends to be the social norm in our time. That moment in *The Wizard of Oz* is not altogether satirical. It is also meant to be emotionally fulfilling. We are supposed to feel very positive about the scarecrow's new image. The message is, "To think positively is sufficient for change. You do not need Grace nor do you need real transformation. Just positive thinking, or believing, about yourself is entirely sufficient." In reality, of course, such "positive thinking" is not sufficient at all.

You are making a gesture now toward the kind of life that you would lead if you were in love with God, if you were emotionally committed to God and emotionally committed to your relationship to me, and if you were rightly established as a religious community. There is a motion in that direction, but it is still only beginning, weak and still tentative and not yet very profound. You tend to generate a kind of self-satisfaction as soon as you make even very minor changes in your life. Thus, the "Wizard-of-Oz principle" is at work. Everybody wants to feel as good about himself (or herself) as he can, and as soon as possible. Since that is everybody's motive, you must be very careful—invariably you play "let's pretend" when it is time for real changes.

I am not the Wizard of Oz. I do not accept your false faces as true practice, as genuine conversion. Thus, you must not forget the emotional nature of this practice. Your consideration must always be emotional. Never allow it to degenerate into "let's pretend" and mere positive affirmation. There must be a real and direct feeling association among devotees and a constant, feeling practice of love-surrender to God, or surrender of the whole bodily being into the Living Principle, the Life-Current, in every moment. You must literally practice this heartfelt surrender at all times, and you must literally oblige one another to this practice.

You should not merely think about emotion every now and then. Your practice must be constantly emotional. What is wrong with these purgative rituals that you enact is that they are periodic. For a few moments you think about emotion, or act as if you are emotional. You may temporarily even appear to be emotional. Then the ritual is over and you are supposed to be a smiling, affirmative character, acting and talking as if you understand everything. How superficial! We are involved by tendency in such a mechanical and worldly way of life that we do not live emotionally. We are like mere salt-of-the-earth workers, plodding our way through life and fulfilling our humble tasks, as if such an existence were the purpose of life.

You must be able to maintain a feeling association with everybody. You must be trustable in your relations altogether, not given to phasing and emotional betrayal. You must literally practice your association with God from the heart, in every moment. Your habit, however, is to put on the false face of self-affirmation and remain self-possessed, absorbed by your emotional problem. The emotional problem manifests fundamentally as self-possession and lack of energy and attention in relationship. When your energy and attention are yielded to self-absorption, then your energy and attention for others and for God seem to be missing. Your self-possession is perfectly obvious to everybody. And, since it is so obvious, the opposite disposition is also obvious—and that is what is required, the obvious practice of a loving, serving life.

These periodic ritual conversations in which you receive your diploma, or are led to think affirmatively that you are a devotee, must end. You must practice from the heart and you must live a serving life. Stop phasing. Stop the endless consideration of the tendency toward unlove, which is the emotional problem that everyone suffers. That consideration never becomes an actual, emotional, whole bodily change and a new way of life. In such a consideration of limitations, you are overwhelmed by one another's weakness. As a result, you decide to accept limitations in one another instead of continuing with the consideration and breaking through the limits and the withholding that you suffer.

The only thing wrong with anyone in any moment of limitation is the collapse of the heart. When the heart collapses, the energies all over the body become distorted. Thus, the transformation of the heart is the single and fundamental occupation of Man at this time in our evolution. A person must directly enter into loving association with the All-Pervading Transcendental Divine Reality and Person, and he (or she) must persist in that form of existence from moment to moment. If he lives in love with God, then naturally he associates with all beings through love. Whatever he is associated with becomes the medium, the Divine Image in fact, for his association with God. Such a one is always associating with God in love. Therefore, all his relationships are loving relationships. Self-transcendence is the quality of his action. He lives as a servant in the highest sense.

The quality of such a devotee's existence is the quality of radiance to others and to God. It is an emotional radiance. It is also full of energy, and it is physical. It is the radiance of energy and attention in relationship. In the company of such a person others feel an endless force of consciousness and energy to which the individual is surrendered bodily and emotionally. Thus, the quality of God, or the spiritual Power that Radiates the worlds, is expressed through such a person quite naturally, and he or she becomes an increasingly different kind of person because of that expression. A community of such people becomes a profoundly unique association of human beings, because they work constantly to transform the emotional and moral dimension that is basic to our existence.

In general we tend not to engage the emotional dimension at all. We avoid it. We play the game of emotional dissociation from the world, from one another, and from God. When we dramatize this problem of emotional dissociation, this quality of the collapse of feeling, energy, and attention, then we become self-servers, totally without clarity in relationship — not only in human relationships, but in all relationships, and in relationship to God most fundamentally. This constant and unconscious effort to create emotional dissociation must be undermined. We serve one another by helping to break this habit and by reestablishing one another in authentic emotional association, in love-surrender to God and a loving, radiant life altogether, in all relations. We must bring down this emotional barrier that exists between us and never again play the game of "let's pretend."

I have heard you talk about your dramatizations.

At times you feel you are living as if on an automatic circuit of tendency, but you feel that you live in God the rest of the time. You must understand that the dramatization of emotional dissociation does not happen only sometimes. The total collapse of the being, the fundamental emotional dissociation, is effective at all times, even when you think you are being positively or energetically emotional in relation to something or someone. Even at those times, if you are sensitive to yourself, you will feel yourself withholding at the root of the emotional gesture. The gesture is not based on love, but it is a superficial activity created by outer circumstances. Sometimes, therefore, your outer circumstances are such that you appear to be a loving person, but in truth you are no more loving than before. You are contracted even then, and you are playing "let's pretend."

You must also recognize the emotional limitations of your upbringing and background in the middle class of the twentieth century West. Most of those who come to me have come out of the middle-class world of slick associations, in which this emotional matter has never been dealt with and the whole affair of spiritual life has never been seriously considered. The term "middle-class world" is just another way of describing the world of "let's pretend." It is a TV world of totally subhuman existence founded in the collapse of emotion into self-possession. We are really referring to that TV society when we self-critically call ourselves "middle-class." We are so superficial, we play "let's pretend" so profoundly, that the reality of TV becomes our own minds.

In the game of "let's pretend," you have a serious confrontation with somebody every now and then, and at the end of it you kiss one another or slap one another on the back. You feel good about one another, but you have not changed at all. You have simply passed through the superficial ritual that is acknowledged as sufficient for friendship and trust in our ordinary society. It is not real friendship, however, not real trust, because each emotional personality is self-possessed.

What I am considering with you is that each of us is most characteristically and basically an emotional personality. But you are not living emotionally, with radiant feeling. You are living in the collapse of emotion, in Narcissism, self-possession, and doubt. Your bodily life is devoted to self-indulgence, and your mental life is devoted to illusions and obsessions, all because there is a collapse at the root, at the emotional being. Furthermore, we all mightily resist making the change from self-possession to God-possession, emotional surrender, and loving service. Therefore, if this Church's community is to represent a unique advantage in the life of an individual, he or she must be party to the agreement that the community represents among those who live in it: constantly to maintain this emotional consideration — in other words, to demand the real, obvious, feeling gesture of the being and accept nothing less as a condition of membership in the community. All the emotional limitations that people bring to one another and that make them untrustworthy must be undone. There must be a demand for emotional association, or right association, in every moment. The slick, affirmative, personality game, the fake piety game, and all the other superficial games that people play must be abandoned as no longer acceptable.

This consideration of the activity of emotional dissociation, or Narcissus, must not be dropped. It is not something that you take seriously only every now and then. It must be constant. You must constantly observe what you are doing at the heart and transcend it. That is what it is to practice the heart in every moment. Therefore, you must be able to inspect the limit on the heart in every moment. You must be able to inspect this process of emotional dissociation, whereby you are always entering into the separative, subjective mood of the separate person, instead of the radiant or loving mood of the devotee, or the true person.

DEVOTEE: I feel that this emotional conversion is not something that I can will to happen.

DA FREE JOHN: That is true, but paradoxically it is also not out of your hands altogether. You are obliged to associate consciously with That with which you are in love. If you spend time in the company of what is lovable, then the emotional radiance of the being, the love that is native to the being, will naturally come forward. Right association is the secret, then. It is said that of all the things a person can do, association with the God-Realized personality, the saint, the Spiritual Master, is the best, simply to be in the company of one who is lovable in the highest sense, one in love with whom the very Force of God is encountered. Emotional conversion is not out of your hands. You are not obliged to wait until it happens to you. It occurs when you are in love in the fullest sense. Therefore, the simplest way to accomplish this change is to spend your time in the company of one with whom you are in love.

The best Company in which to spend all your time is the Company of God and the Spiritual Master. There are other relationships in which you are also in love, but the relationships with God and the Spiritual Master are primary. True religion is simply a matter of maintaining association with God and with the Spiritual Master moment to moment. Then the natural emotion, or the force of love, devotion, and self-surrender, will tend to be evoked by that Company. Thus, devotees are instructed to recite the Name of God, to remember God constantly, to hold the image of the Spiritual Master in their minds, to talk about the Spiritual Master, to praise the Spiritual Master, and to think of the Spiritual Master. These are all ways of maintaining Divine Association. The secret of ecstatic practice is to find your way of maintaining association with the One who is lovable, or the Beloved, in every moment.

How do you do that? Such practice is the artfulness required of you in every moment. You must create this theatre of Divine Association in relation to God and to me. Your emotional conversion is not outside your power to effect. You must practice, and practice is something you must do. This is how you do it: Rather than willfully trying to conjure up the emotion of love, you must understand yourself and maintain total

43

psycho-physical association with the One with Whom you are in love in the fullest spiritual sense—in other words, with God. You must choose to do this. You must come to this point of clarity in yourself, wherein you realize that to practice this Divine Association is all that life is. Everything else is an expression of what life is when it fails to be that.

You must be committed to this practice, and of course this practice makes you a saint! This is how you must transcend your middle-class, street personality, and you naturally will transcend it if you will practice as I am suggesting, in this emotional sense. If you will serve in love constantly, if you will constantly and literally serve God in every moment—not God as an idea, but God confronted as the very Presence of Life—then your street personality will naturally fall away. It will be transformed into the higher personality or character. It is a matter of remaining alive in the emotional sense, moment to moment, without recoil from relationship, without emotional collapse of feeling and attention onto the self. Do not let anybody tell you that he or she cannot do this. And do not let anybody tell you that he or she is doing it if it is perfectly obvious to your feeling that he or she is not!

Live in the Spirit of Surrender

DA FREE JOHN: You must not have the idea that to be a devotee is to be constantly observing your negative patterns and problems and having insight into them. That is not the practice — that is definitely <u>not</u> the practice! That attitude will simply cause you to manufacture endless negative patterns to observe and manipulate and penetrate with insight. Your business is not to have problems in order to have insights. That is not the way of life I am suggesting.

Certainly you must consider your existence and "hear" the Teaching and "see" the Spiritual Master and come to a point of commitment to the Way of Life. But you are supposed to have already listened to the critical argument of the Teaching to the point of "hearing"; you are to be here as a devotee who lives moment to moment surrender to God from the heart. The Way of Life of such a person is not constantly to observe his negative patterns. He considers, enters into, inspects the whole mechanics of his conventional life, but he is not in any sense living a conventional life anymore. He is a devotee. He is practicing surrender to God from the heart. He surrenders in every moment, not just at times of formal devotional practice. Formal devotional and sacramental occasions are times of learning, cultural moments, a way of intensifying the quality of your higher adaptation, but for the devotee there is nothing singular or unique about formal devotional practices in the scheme of ordinary life.

Fundamentally the practice is a moment to moment discipline in direct confrontation with the Living Reality. Either you live contracted, as Narcissus, or you live surrendered as the devotee. You can either live in the natural state that is prior to reaction to the pattern of things, or you can live the reaction itself. Having considered it, which will you choose? If you choose to surrender, then surrender is your business, not watching your negative patterns. Why should you be waiting to observe negative patterns? And why should negative patterns be significant? As a devotee you live to be in love, to live in love with God—that is existence for you. You must live in that spirit with everyone then. You must create real agreements and simplify your life in the areas where complication is just confusion, and you must transform your life altogether into something great through most perfect surrender to God moment to moment — and you must be able to trust everybody with whom you live to do that also.

Therefore, not only must you be converted, but you must also consider and study and make right use of the traditional recommendations of how to spend time in the Company of the Spiritual Master. The fundamental Principle of spiritual life that has been communicated by all Masters of the past is that the best thing to do is to spend time in the Company of a God-Realized person. How do you honor that Principle if you are converted to God? How do you honor it explicitly? The expression of your relationship to me is utterly an expression of your relationship to God and to this Way of Life. Therefore, the first relationship that you must transform is the one you have to me. It is in this Company, in your association with me, that you are becoming converted. You must not only "hear" me but also "see" me. You must recognize me in this very Company and presume a right relationship with me. That recognition is just as necessary as the fundamental conversion; in fact it is the same thing. A right relationship to me is necessary before you will be able to enter truly into right agreements in your other relations —first in your marriage, then in your household, then in your community, then in your relations with the world.

47

In the West we have the idea that even though Man may receive the Revelation of God, nevertheless he always fails to act as one who has faith, who Communes with God, who is God-Realized. Westerners do not comprehend the power of Grace, the power of mere association with God![1] That Divine Association is the Truth, the gospel, and it may be realized directly, intimately, bodily. Divine Association heals and transforms. Thus, there is no inherent disposition in Man to renounce that Association. But Man, including all of you, is profoundly lazy. It does not seem to you now that you have any choice in how you may live, but you absolutely do have a choice. Yes, you are convicted of sinfulness, but you can be converted in your heart and you can relate to me in an entirely different manner. You can create a Sanctuary and a Church that has great strength. And you can live a true life and grow spiritually. You can do all of this instead of everything that you are tending to do.

1. For a more complete discussion of this idea, see "The Religious Ambivalence of Western Man" in *The Way That I Teach*.

48

Our considerations together should reach a point of Revelation, presumption, true practice. However, we will realize that Revelation only through the emotional transformation of individuals. How will you relate to your spouse, to your children, to your household, to our total community, to the world? The conversion that is obliged upon you is not the same as deciding to believe in Jesus. The conversion to which you are obliged will change everything about you, change all of your actions. Emotional conversion requires such changes. Therefore, you must change your lives and this Church altogether. It will be perfectly obvious what you must do when you are converted.

Allow Your Life to Be God's Business

D A FREE JOHN: You are disturbed, you are uptight, you are not surrendered bodily, and you are working on internal programs for ultimate surrender. The truth is that you are simply afraid, not surrendered. Those programs are what you do when you do not surrender emotionally, when you cannot see that you are simply contracting and cannot release the contraction and allow whatever is happening to happen. You must trust the process of your own life, whether it is to go mad, to become ill, to work, to succeed, or to die. Be free of fear. Surrender to the Person of God, the actual Living God. Trust the Divine altogether. Give yourself up emotionally to God. Do it to the point that the physically based fear of death vanishes on the basis of trust alone. Practice complete devotion and absolute surrender. Do not just tread the path of gradual attainment in your emotional and ceremonial approaches to God. Give yourself up completely in this moment. Give up everything at every depth and in every area of your life. Allow life to be the theatre of God, in which what seems to be appropriate and necessary in your case will be accomplished spontaneously. Allow all of life to be God's business. Whatever arises, high or low, such a life will simply be surrendering to the point of happiness, giving up to God completely. If you will do what I urge you to do, then this instruction is sufficient. You do not really need to know all the technicalities of yoga and the cosmic subtleties of the higher planes of the phenomenal worlds. You need not know anything. You need not become convinced of anything except that you are suffering a contracted state of existence. Feel the force of that contraction, its emotional force, its physical force. Feel the quality of contraction and realize that it is your own action. Realize that you can exist in a totally different condition merely by recognizing your own separative activity and transcending it in each moment. Just surrender emotionally and completely.

Serve God and Live on Grace

D A FREE JOHN: Practitioners of this Way serve the Spiritual Master and they serve God. You must perform this service with your life—and you must learn how to do it in the form of all your activities so that every action is God-Communion. When you are at home in bed with your husband or wife, you must conduct your loving as sacramental service to the Spiritual Master. Literally! You must live your sexual intimacy directly as Communion with the Presence of God. *Sexual communion* [1] is a living and profound matter. It changes you bodily. Everything about it is new and transforming. It is not the same as taking time out for a little believing — it is ecstatic practice in that moment. You must learn how to adapt to God and to the Spiritual Master in all of your living, to allow every moment to be literally a form of bodily worship. Every moment must be a moment of true feeling, Divine emotion, not all of the self-possessed motivations that you call feelings and that are only the garbage of your own Narcissistic life.

For these reasons, you see, the principle that all service is meditation on the Spiritual Master is worthy of significant consideration. All service is direct service to God. When such service is true of you, you are serving and loving others, but not in conventional terms. You are serving on the basis of this native,

---

1. For a complete discussion of *sexual communion* see *Love of the Two-Armed Form*, by Da Free John.

essential response, this Radiance that pervades your own being through sacrifice of self-possession and reactive emotion. Naturally, then, everyone whom you serve is felt to arise in God. You serve everyone in your sacramental service to God through the Spiritual Master. Everything that you do from moment to moment must therefore be considered in formal terms. What does your action become as a sacramental act? To what degree is it failing to fulfill the formal obligations of devotion? What must you do in this moment to make your every action a full and direct service to the Spiritual Master and to God — literal Divine Association, ecstatic association, literal feeding on the Divine, literal Fullness in God?

Giving gifts to God is literal service to God. Thus, it must not be merely a technical affair. It is intended to be literal sacrifice. "Prasad," or the Divine Gift that you receive in return, is the abundance left over from your sacrifice, that which God does not require, not because God has no connection to it and thus it falls to you, but because it is excess, superfluity upon which you live. Give up everything, surrender everything, release your hold on everything, and, without concerns, receive whatever is given by Grace. Live on Grace, not as a passive person in the world but as one who is not concerned in the world. The devotee is not just waiting around for something good, or something bad, to happen to him. He is active but free of concern, because he is always surrendered.

PART II

The Sacred Emotional Commitment to Sexual Love

Talks to devotees

One who is a lover in God sees only the Divine Life expressed in and as the one he or she loves. When Life is recognized to be the Truth of the loved-one, then Life becomes the Loved-One. Thus, it is just such recognition of Life in the form of one's lover and the process of sexual relationship that makes true love possible and relieves the relationship of morbid self-possession, jealousy, binding attachment, and romantic illusions. Those who embrace the Divine in psycho-physical ecstasy of all kinds transcend self and other and are always already free in God.

Da Free John
Love of the Two-Armed Form

The Pleasure of God-Communion
Must Exceed the Pleasure of Sex

DA FREE JOHN: It is interesting to consider the difference, in terms of actual feeling and enjoyment, between your association with sex and your association with God. Your involvement with sex is much more elaborate, complex, absorbing, and continuous, and it is associated with more pleasure. One of the complications of your present state is that you simply have not learned or adapted to the intense physical and personal pleasure of God-Communion — at least not in comparison with all the other things to which you have adapted pleasurably. Very little actual association with God is as pleasurable to you as sexual enjoyment, or eating, or the other games of daily life. Your association with God is almost empty in comparison with the complicated associations of pleasure and pain that you have with everything else. Not having lived as a devotee of God all your life, you show the signs of somebody who has not yet learned how to enjoy association with God.

You may have observed that during sexual intercourse you become self-possessed, you dissociate yourself emotionally. The feeling dimension of your being collapses and you become concentrated in mere physical sensation. Under such circumstances you view emotion or feeling as just a way to make sex more "fun." You may even think that you are "adding" God-Communion to the event, but really you are only adding pleasure to your own sexual involvement. Such self-manipulation is not the same as self-transcending love. Thus, you see, you suffer emotionally during sexual intercourse.

Entering into pleasurable Communion with God is part of our necessary consideration of sexuality. Our association with God should be equally as pleasurable as sexual play, even more pleasurable because it is continuous and it involves the entire body, including the mechanisms that you exploit in sexual play. Thus, surrender to God is more pleasurable than sexual play, even in ordinary bodily terms.

You simply do not yet know how to surrender, you see. You have not learned it. Meanwhile, you are troubled by what you have already learned, the inclinations you have by tendency! That is the trouble with learning sex before you learn devotion: Thereafter it is difficult to cultivate devotion, because you cannot feel good about devotion itself in the face of this intense pleasure of sex. Sex is a familiar and pleasurable distraction, whereas God-Association is not so familiar and seems to require a certain period of learning during which you do not feel as blissful as you would like.

This consideration of the ecstasy of God-love is just beginning in you. You are still only considering being ecstatic rather than actually involving yourself in this moment in the fierce, direct confrontation with God. You are still only thinking of self-improvement. You speak and act like people who are obsessed with and somehow consoled by this world. You see, then, what is required of you in order to take up this Way of Life. You cannot be naive about yourself. You cannot be full of yourself. There is so much to be transformed, so much to realize, that you must give up all resistance, all wishing that from now on you could be the perfect devotee without having to learn or suffer or sacrifice. You would like this Way to be consoling — but it is not. Yes, you can enter directly into ecstasy in this moment — but only through perfect sacrifice. Your moment to moment existence must be the heartfelt practice of literal sacrifice, service, and surrender, and it must be performed with great intelligence. This Way of devotional surrender cannot be mere emotional good-heartedness. No, you must be intelligent about your practice, and you must make your God-Communing life as intensely pleasurable and blissful as all the other things that now distract you.

God-Communion is the primary bodily pleasure. It is simply that you have not realized it as such, and, therefore, you conceive of God-Communion as self-limiting and ascetic. You think you will engage some form of asceticism a little bit at a time and without practicing fiercely, and that eventually, as a result, you will realize God. You tend to feel that God-Realization is a matter of stripping yourselves of attachments, relations, and enjoyments, rather than giving up to God. However, in truth God-Communion has nothing to do with such self-denial. It is a matter of outshining attachments, relations, and enjoyments through Communion with the Primal Enjoyment. If you are already in a condition of spiritual, bodily enjoyment, then all manifest enjoyments become superficial, ordinary, conventional processes that are neither overwhelming nor binding.

We were talking recently about St. Francis.

Whenever he felt worldly desires, he would mutilate himself, punish the body for desiring. Once he threw himself into a briar patch. On another occasion he threw himself naked into the sea to cool off his cravings. Rather than living in the principle of God-Communion, he was busy working against desire. He associated with troublesome desires for which he could not be sanely responsible. He felt that they were happening to him. Thus, he could deal with them only in this bizarre, ritualistic, strategic fashion, trying to tear himself away from their binding force.

In contrast to St. Francis, others spend their whole lives indulging sexual desire. But neither the solution of indulgence nor the solution of suppression, as we see in St. Francis, is illumined. Neither of these two tendencies in any individual is true in itself — everyone adapts in some way to both solutions. Therefore, this matter of the emotional conversion, of the spiritual transcendence of all experience, is the root of the consideration of sexuality and the root of daily life for all practitioners of this Way. When the emotional conversion is not realized moment to moment, all practice becomes mediocre, if not simply false.

The Mood of Betrayal

DA FREE JOHN: You are associated with sexuality as a self-generated, self-possessed, universal impulse. By "universal" I mean that almost anyone and anything can become the object of this impulse. Anything can become erotically interesting to you because your attention radiates in all directions, self-generated, self-possessed, and self-possessing. Ultimately, desire is something that you are doing to yourself. Thus, it does not make any difference with whom or with what you have stimulating sexual association. You are doing it and you are doing it <u>to</u> yourself. As long as you remain in this self-possessed condition, generating sexuality for the sake of your own sense of pleasurable immunity, your attention is simply radiating in all directions through this interest. You casually associate sexually with anyone who comes along. At the same time you try to be married despite this emotional problem (which is a spiritual problem). You try to be true to one another, to have loving, undistracted attention for one another. Yet neither of you is involved with sex as anything but a self-generated, self-possessed, universal desire — and you cannot confine a universal desire.

This dilemma is an expression of the Narcissistic character, the self-possessed, self-defensive, vulnerable, threatened personality, the one who knows he can be rejected, that he can suffer from separation, and that he can die. That one, that emotional problem, separate from God, feeling alone, feeling threatened altogether, is also involved in sex. That one is you in your unil-lumined position, and the person with whom you are most intimate is in <u>exactly</u> the same position. He or she too is self-possessed, trying to protect himself or her-self, fearing to love and surrender, fearing the loss of his or her lover, feeling the potential betrayal that the other represents. Thus, in the usual person the motive of sexual love is never fully satisfied or concentrated in a single relationship, and his or her sexual interest re-mains universal, casual, self-possessed, and self-generated, never truly expressed in relationship and never a free impulse, always associated with self-possessed or self-possessing fear.

If you will honestly discuss your sexual relation-ship, you will find that each of you is fundamentally suffering in the mood of betrayal, of having been be-trayed and always feeling that you are about to be be-trayed. You will discover in your discussion with one another that both of you in some very essential way are promiscuous characters whose emotional maturity is equal to that of very young, reactive, adolescent, or even infantile personalities. Therefore, you cannot re-ally trust one another, nor do you really trust yourselves altogether. Somehow you sense that love cannot be what this relationship is fundamentally all about.

The closer you look at one another in this discus-sion of your sexuality the more anxious you will be-come, the more you will exaggerate your characteristic negative reaction. You will go on and on and on in your discussion—and you really must go through it to the end; you must talk about all of your promiscuous thoughts, actions, and feelings, past, present, and possibly future. You must confess all of that to one another. But after you have gone on with this confessing and essentially come to the end of your information, what are you going to do? By that time you may have completely disturbed and aggravated one another with all this negative content. You may have no sympathy at all for one another anymore! You will certainly know that you are both weak characters, obviously sexually fascinated with other people, seeming to be entirely committed to your negative cycle of emotional reactivity and your self-protective games. And now you are confronted with all of this information, the whole problem, this situation that does not justify love and surrender to one another.

You have probably also begun to become a little weirdly fascinating to one another. Even though you do not want to be betrayed or abandoned by your mate, you begin to imagine him or her in sexual encounters with other people. Your situation begins to take on the quality of an erotic movie. There is something you like about the promiscuous energy of your mate, even though you do not like its ultimate implications. You may even start to play off one another sexually in this consideration. Your sexual consideration might go on endlessly in this fashion without ever becoming conclusive. What are you going to do? You could say, "We will not do this anymore." And you may even try the traditional solutions: "I will wear a veil whenever I come into the room." But such solutions are not ultimately effective.

Thus, you must be able to carry the consideration beyond this point. You are dealing with this matter as

64

if it were a sexual problem, but it is fundamentally an emotional problem. Once you are emotionally straight, once you are converted at the heart, then sexuality becomes something entirely different. Therefore, your emotional conversion must be the next point of your discussion. Perhaps you must abandon the sexual discussion for a while and talk to one another in emotional terms. You must tell one another what you feel your basic emotional state is from moment to moment. You must feel and confess that you are basically a fearful person, afraid of rejection, that the emotionally negative and reactive state is essentially characteristic of you. Until you are cured in your heart, any discussion about sexuality will drive you mad.

As a result of your adaptation and experiences, you are all in an emotionally wounded state. Since you are emotionally weak, subject to emotional reactivity and all kinds of self-possessed motives, there is no way that you can have a pure and free and loving marriage. There will always be a promiscuous dimension to it, a casual, erotic quality of association, that will always exist as a threat. In other words, in your present disposition love will never be simply true of you, and you will never be healed at the heart. This sexual problem will persist because you are self-possessed, and sex unillumined by love is simply a universal urge. It is only when the heart and therefore the whole body-mind is healed in true emotional conversion to the love relationship to God that you can accept the body-mind as the form of your manifestation and live all of its functions sanely and happily and with a will.

We each want our lover to be able to say to us, "I

love only you and desire only you forever. I have never desired anyone the way I desire you. I have never felt this way about anyone other than you." Yet knowing that it cannot be true makes you feel a little negative, even terribly negative, about life. It confirms your reasons for despair. Anyone can have pleasurable sexual relations with anyone else, and with almost any thing, for that matter. If you were to simply live in your emotional problem, just given up to universal desire, you might try to have pleasurable sexual relations with everyone and everything in the world. Those you would not actually take to bed you would want to take to bed. And you would be obsessed and tormented constantly by your own sexual habit.

65

Fundamentally, you must be changed in your being, in your heart, in your feeling. Until then you are not only weak and reactive, but you never even learn the lesson about the will. Until then you waver in your practice, and your attention wanders casually everywhere, randomly distracted, fascinated, and stimulated. Promiscuity is what you all have practiced until now, you see. You have given yourself up to forms of weak-willed practice. As a result you represent only weak-minded patterns and you are possessed by your various functions and inclinations. You use every one of them as a way to dramatize neurotic, self-possessed motives and all the qualities of a threatened personality. Thus, you must become capable of practicing love with a will, of concentrating energy and attention in relationship, and of making changes in your action and your circumstances. But you cannot willfully become changed in your feeling. Feeling is primary, greater than the will. Therefore, you must be healed in your feeling being. You must be converted in your feeling. Love must be true of you.

To the degree that love is not true of you, that love of God is not true of you, you will realize only your sinful life. You will continue in your wavering of attention, your fearful, threatened, self-possessed life. It will be necessary, therefore, that you experience a great philosophical circle before coming to the simple recognition that there are two things that you can do in any moment. You can either contract in the midst of what arises, or you can release. There are only those two actions. You are never involved in anything else — either the knot of self-possession or surrender, the avoidance of relationship or love. There is nothing else.

Yet in your marriage you want to carry on a mad debate with one another. You blithely imagine that your spouse could communicate to you that he or she is without casual, erotic thoughts. What do you really think your spouse is like? Your spouse is just like you. Neither one of you is free in your heart. Neither one of you is truly converted to God, essentially given up to God-love from moment to moment. You are self-possessed, reactive, threatened, afraid of rejection, afraid of death, and afraid of separation. You are suffering. People who suffer are liable to make all the destructive decisions that sinful, self-possessed people make. Therefore, your spouse is never going to have anything perfect to tell you about himself or herself. Neither of you will be able to confess love unless you can be healed in your emotion, prior to the will and thinking and experiencing and all the rest of it.

You must be healed in your fundamental nature. You must be healed of this contraction, this recoil, this fear, this threatened sense of self, in which you exploit yourself to give yourself whatever feeling of pleasure you can acquire. You will betray everyone for that sensation. Thus, in some sense, even though this recoil or dissociation may not appear in some exaggerated way in a given moment, it is certainly arising in the most fundamental sense in your consciousness, body, and heart moment to moment. You are recoiled from Life, Life-negative, Narcissistic, self-possessed.

67

You will never satisfy one another with statements like, "I love only you and I desire only you." That line of discussion never comes to an end. Somehow, by the end of this consideration, you must become expressed to one another as love for one another, which is senior to tendencies and sensations and impulses. Thereafter, that love will be the focus of your concentration in life with one another. From the point of view of that love, there is no question of promiscuity or anything like it, because the association of love is the true and constant form of your intercourse with one another. You must come to that point. If you cannot, you personally are still possessed by an emotional problem that you cannot transcend.

DEVOTEE: When my husband and I come to rest with one another, when we can simply look at one another without all our other personal complications, I feel a profound connection to him. The problem is that I continually return to my usual pattern.

DA FREE JOHN: The profound connection you feel in that moment is the only sense whatsoever in which you are married. There is no other portion of your entire body-mind or emotion that is married to your husband. He is just another moment in your whole game of associations.

DEVOTEE: Such moments keep me attracted to him.

DA FREE JOHN: What a pity that you feel that only at times! Marriage is the practice of abiding in that emotional commitment in every moment. You cannot do that until you are free in your emotion. Your "hearing" of the Teaching must be an emotional awakening, and your "seeing" of the Spiritual Master must be an emotional realization, not the reading of intellectual and ordinary verbal signs. True life is a matter of the heart.

DEVOTEE: It seems that such a Way of life can be realized only through practicing a feeling relationship with the Divine Person.

DA FREE JOHN: Yes, but is the Divine Person altogether obvious to you?

DEVOTEE: No.

DA FREE JOHN: Well, then! How can you practice this feeling relationship with the Divine Person? What you are describing is like falling in love with your wife before you ever see her!

You are in a mood of bad faith. You have fallen

out of love with everything—out of love with God, out of love with the Divine Reality. Your experiences have impressed you gravely, you see. They have made you self-conscious and doubtful. Thus, you have only minimal energy for love and positive association because you have despaired. Yes, you can practice aspects of the disciplines of this Way with a will. But that effort will be always relatively superficial in its effects until you have been transformed in your feeling consideration of your very existence, until you have fallen out of this pattern of bad faith relative to the totality of things, until you have stopped avoiding relationship or contracting upon yourself and are simply released to the Living Reality. You will not be able to transform the relative mediocrity of your relationship with your spouse until you deal with this contraction. Until you are healed emotionally, simply, you will not be able to enter into right emotional relations with other beings.

There must be a fundamental restoration of natural love, trust, openness, surrender to the Living World, the Living Reality, the Living Being. Such love must become natural to you. Now what is natural to you is to be contracted, to be afraid. You are emotionally upset already. Is that the way it is supposed to be? You had better find out altogether, not just intellectually but in your feeling. Until you are free in your feeling, you can never be trusted in relationship, you cannot concentrate in relationship, you are scattered everywhere in your attention.

Lust Is an Emotion

D A FREE JOHN: Sexual feeling for someone is completely a matter of your responsibility. Because it is an automaticity in you, however, you think it is something that happens to you. But it is a self-generated automaticity that you constantly trigger to make yourself feel better.

Sexual love arises quite naturally in the intimacy we enjoy with the one to whom we are married. There is no other relationship quite like marriage. Thus, in one who is in love with God, surrendered, and always capable of love in human relations, sexuality is not a universal desire. It is a functional enjoyment and extension of happiness that arises only in the intimacy permitted with one's spouse. It is not random. Such a person is not involved exclusively with the sex function in any case. He (or she) exists fundamentally in ecstatic Communion with God. The marriage relationship is a matter of love and the expression of love and nothing else. What other form of relationship is possible with your spouse, or with anyone else for that matter? If you are a devotee, you live as Love-Communion. Whatever your sexual relationship turns out to be is simply the case for you, and so be it!

Therefore, the first thing you must do is transcend lust. You need not renounce sex if you can fulfill it in love, as *sexual communion*. But it will never be sexual communion in your case if you remain a lustful personality, an essentially loveless and therefore unsurrendered, self-possessed personality. You cannot be lustful

and enter into sexual communion. You cannot be lustful and be truly married. You cannot promise your
constant attention and fidelity if you are a lustful person, because you cannot feel that such a commitment is
yours to offer. You do not really believe that sexual
attention is under your control. You think you are
possessed by a demonic sexual force. In some sense that
is true — but it is <u>your</u> lustfulness. You are <u>self</u>-
possessed.

Your self-possession is your own concern. It cannot be relieved magically. Thus, the ultimate gesture
of transcendence is necessarily yours. Grace attracts you
to Itself with great force, but if you are repelled, if you
do not surrender, then you will take a great deal of time
to become free. Therefore, you must fundamentally
realize in your marriage relationship that lust must be
transcended in the commitment to marriage itself. You
cannot enter into the marriage relationship in order to
fulfill lustful intentions. Lust inevitably destroys the
union of marriage.

You must emerge from the cave of self-possession,
and you must be converted from lust. You have lived
your sexuality in a random and self-possessed fashion all
your life, so that what you feel as sexual desiring is
essentially lustful. You may not think of it as lust—you
may think of it as normal desire—but you lust for its
satisfaction. You are constantly desiring, considering
sexual fulfillment, and presenting yourself as a lustful
personality at least psychologically, inwardly, subjec-
tively, and in some outwardly sexual way as well. You
are driven by sexual lust, possessed and disturbed by it.
Eventually if this sexual craving is not sufficiently satis-

fied, you become extremely unstable emotionally.

You will notice that when you are lustful, you are disturbed emotionally. If you exploit yourself sexually beyond your usual intention to fulfill desire, you become obsessed by the fulfillment itself. You become hyped by it, exaggerated, even more lustful. If you become sensitive to it, you will also observe that lustfulness hurts. It is desperate. Lustfulness does not love, it is never satisfied, and it is always betraying relationships.

Thus, the problems that appear in your marriage are problems of lust, and lust is invariably accompanied by unlove, or self-possession—the constant wondering if one is loved, the unwillingness to be love, the constant feeling that one is betrayed, or about to be betrayed. Instead of worrying about being betrayed, you must be more certain that you are not betraying your spouse.

If you are lustful, you have thousands of lovers, inevitably, all the ones in your mind, your memory, and your daily association. All the shapes that flash around in your unconscious mind, and all the driven need and the easy access to sexual titillation mutilate your relations and your intimacies and cause you to betray them. You constantly complain, for example, about your lack of sexual fulfillment. You do not necessarily say to your husband or wife, "I'd like to be sexually fulfilled!" — but you punish your spouse in all kinds of other ways, in thousands of daily episodes of emotional reactivity, endless betrayals and failures to serve and love simply. You mutilate your spouse out of sexual failure and frustration. You are dominated by sex, rather than being the master of sex through love.

Your marriage relationship must be characterized by love and freedom from obsession and lust, but willful celibacy is neither appropriate nor sufficient for people like you. Something more than such a mechanical choice is required. You must realize a complete transformation of the sexual dimension of your life so that it is utterly free of lust and practiced only as an expression of love in your intimate marital relationship. That is the complete and total end of the matter. That is how you must practice sexuality, and that is all it amounts to. Beyond sex there is all the rest of the totality of existence, with which you must enter into heartfelt association.

Lust, you see, is an emotion and an obsession. Therefore, it is like an emotional problem, a form of unlove, like any other kind of sin. Lust is an emotional drive that completely absorbs us when we are overcome by it and prevents the heart from radiating the emotion of love. Lust is a limit on the heart. Thus, you must be free of the emotion that is lust. Such freedom is possible only if you surrender to God, live as love, and serve your spouse in love, never permitting what is sexual to complicate or undermine the love-relationship. In such a disposition you can fulfill the sexual impulse in that relationship with the frequency and the quality or intensity that is natural to you in love, rather than in lust. Then, you can enter into a simple and true intimacy with one another.

To be free of lust is not to be nonsexual. You must discover the difference. Sexual love is free. It is not binding, not obsessive like lust. Sexual love arises totally within the play of truly intimate relationship, and therefore it cannot arise casually.

DEVOTEE: You are right about the painfulness of lust. And it is so serious. It also feels violent, especially promiscuous lust.

DA FREE JOHN: Lust is like Nature, not like Man, you see. In Nature there is no humor at all! In Nature everything is very serious. Lust has that same serious quality. Love in a sexual relationship, or sex in a love relationship, is not really serious. Anything serious is a depression of feeling and delight and humor.

DEVOTEE: It is interesting, Master, that in the *Bhagavad Gita,* Krishna says, "Lust may arise in the mind of the seer, but he is not disturbed by it." I have never really understood until now why lust could continue to arise in the sage. Lust is present in him as Nature, but he does not presume it as a limit.

DA FREE JOHN: Lust has no power to transform him in any fundamental way because, acknowledging his own weakness, he practices only one thing: continuous love of God and, therefore, the confession of the practice of love in all his relations. Love is the one thing to practice, and you must do it with profound intensity. You must simply come to terms with this consideration. You must become saints, you see. Stop deluding yourself and everybody else about how ordinary and out-of-control you are. Become saints, because you must in every moment simply love and surrender to God.

How can you propose anything else to me? You must stop rejecting this higher idea of yourself because of your lust. Your lustfulness prevents you from becoming elegant. It makes you continue to be ordinary and mediocre, whereas you must at least become saints! However, if you cannot commit yourself from the heart to God, you will also not be able to relieve your marriage or your life or yourself or your spouse of lust and all the problems of lust. They will not disappear by any means other than this commitment. You cannot truly be married, you cannot promise or represent the possibility of fidelity, unless you are a devotee, unless you are committed to the Way of love. You must practice that Way so profoundly in your feeling from moment to moment that it totally transforms your life. That is the great creative adventure.

Do you imagine that you can surrender to God and feel lust at the same time? If you do, it is because you do not recognize lust as a form of contracted feeling, as a limit on the heart. When you are being lustful you can imagine, perhaps, that you are also somehow loving. But you are not. You cannot love, because lust is a self-possessed, negative emotion. That is why it is universally declared to be a form of sin. Lust is not love, it is not Radiance, it is not surrender to Infinity, to the Living God. Lust cannot be coincident with God-Communion. You must understand that and be transformed in your sexuality by persisting in love of God and surrender to God.

There is no fixed rule such as, "Now you should be celibate." No. Enter into your sexual intimacy in love, free of lust entirely. Surrender to God all the while, and see what sexual intimacy becomes then. Stop threatening one another with your lustfulness and acting as if you are an irresponsible person who cannot promise to love and to maintain sexual fidelity with your spouse. You can certainly be a true husband or wife if you will simply love your spouse, if you will practice as a lover of God in every moment, in love with God and in love with your spouse. Surrender, sacrifice yourself, serve in those relations, and forget about being troubled by your sin. Your lustfulness has no force if you will simply remember to love, whole bodily, in the moment that lust arises. You will see that lust is transformed, its energy is converted and distributed to the whole body, and it becomes Fullness.

DEVOTEE: Master, it is remarkable how insatiable lust is. A person may have the sense that if he could play out his lust it would disappear. But it is obvious that it does not.

DA FREE JOHN: That is the way we talk when we are obsessed. We are frantic for an almost mystical fulfillment through sex, you see. We actually give up our lives to it, because we refuse to be ecstatic simply and directly. We are refusing to make the essential response of our being in every moment, which is to be surrender and love rather than contraction and fear. We have the choice, so why be the reaction to Life? Be what is already the case. Become philosophical on that basis, rather than on the basis of this doubting, contracted,

self-possessed personality. See what becomes obvious
and true when you depend on Grace. Give yourself to
God. Receive the Living and Transforming Power.
Never forget to do it. Stop troubling your spouse with
all this lustfulness. Let your whole body be converted
by loving and be liberated from all of its sinfulness.
This is the greatest yoga, the foundation yoga of Divine
Communion.

77

Communion with the Universal Current of Life
via the central nervous system, which is fundamental to
our true existence, is obstructed by all of our automaticities. All the inward-directed and outward-
directed qualities of the autonomic nervous system and
all the levels of energy in the central nervous system are
obstructed.[1] The entire psycho-physical circuitry is
obstructed, out of balance, contracted. As long as this
is so, we can never realize the Purity and absolute Bliss
of our essential Existence. Because we are expressed
downward and outward in our earthly lives, we cannot
experience the reverse cycle at a very high psycho-
physical level. As soon as a little Life-Energy begins to
rise in us, we think we are already God-Realized and we
throw off that energy in the next sexual encounter!
Presently you wonder if God exists, or you are terrified
that you are going to die—you are full of complaints.
You are not in love with God at all. You are upset. You
are a sinner, you see — literally! You are literally a
sinner, turned away from God, missing the mark, emotionally upset in the face of the Infinite. Are you not?

1. For a complete discussion of the autonomic and central nervous
systems see *The Enlightenment of the Whole Body*, by Da Free John, chapter 7.

You do not know very much, and you are angry about many things, especially your own inevitable death.

In your marriage, you must become free of lust, and simply love one another, and practice sexuality as sexual communion in the economy that truly serves your Life. But fundamentally you must live the ecstasy of Love-Communion with the Living God. You must practice it, you must be committed to it, and you must be an absolutely stable, absolutely trustworthy, absolutely loving person through that commitment. If you are a woman, you must absolutely be your husband's wife. No doubt about it—he should not have to spend one more day talking with you about your lust. If you are a man, you must be a husband absolutely, with no doubt whatsoever about it. You must not even secretly be involved in or even entertain the possibility of an erotic, lustful life.

Who knows how often the genital embrace will occur if you can persist simply in love, and if you can allow sexuality to be transformed in whatever way it is transformed when you love! Maybe, eventually, you just stop having sex—or maybe not. There is no need to worry about the frequency of sex because there is no prescription for it. But if you simply persist in this Divine love and sexual communion, perhaps the actual physical embrace falls away from your relationship. In any case, you must allow yourself to find out.

PART III

Choose What You Will Do

Talks to devotees

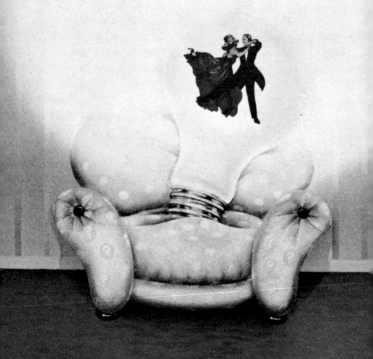

You must choose God. That is the principle. You must enter into absorbed Communion and Happiness in God, the Living Reality. If you will do that, then you will quite naturally bring order to your inclinations, because you already feel good. And the happier you become, the less you are involved in trying to make yourself feel good. God becomes sufficient. It is only when God becomes sufficient and absolutely Real and your absorption becomes perfect and ecstatic that you are lifted out of this absurd and insane situation in which we live.

Da Free John
The Eating Gorilla Comes in Peace

Will You Surrender,
or Will You Contract?

DA FREE JOHN: Will you surrender to the Reality in which you are arising, or will you defend yourself for the rest of your life? Will you contract, will you withdraw, withhold, dissociate, separate, turn upon yourself? Will you avoid all relations, contract from them? Will you react, or will you simply remain in the natural position prior to that recoil? Will you be present? Will you not avoid relationship? Will you shine as love to Infinity? Will you enter into complete Fullness of feeling relative to that Condition in which you are arising? Will you do that as a principle of existence, rather than what you are tending to do, which is to contract upon yourself and become afraid?

The recoil is the action that you perform, and it contains all suffering. But if you persistently remain present in relationship, then you begin to develop a different mind, you create a different form of life, and you become subject to a new understanding, a new Revelation. You begin to recognize the mere Presence of God. You begin to enjoy transformation of your conventional state by Divine Grace.

You are suffering, you see, from all kinds of contraction or self-possessed conditions of the body-mind. You suffer complex versions of these contractions. You suffer because you have persisted as if you had chosen to contract in the midst of Infinity, to hold on to yourself, to live as though threatened. If you can see that such a gesture is false in principle, and if you can choose the

fundamental disposition of surrender, the natural disposition that is open to or continuous with the Condition in which you are arising — if you can choose that
disposition in principle, then in all the aspects of your
complex life you will see the possibility of another
gesture than the one you tend to live in any moment.
You will observe that everything you tend to do is a
form of this contraction rather than of surrender, love,
or free feeling-attention. You live now as if you have an
emotional problem, as if you cannot love and surrender
to the Living Reality and allow yourself to be lived and
transformed as It is clearly intending. You will live
altogether differently, however, once you have committed yourself to another principle than that of contraction, or self-possession, and fear. If you can, in
principle, choose surrender into the Condition in
which you are arising, then all of your acts and
thoughts and reactions will become obsolete, and you
will have a totally new life to which to adapt.

When we recently began an emotional consideration between spouses, we presumed that you each had
already "heard" the Teaching of Truth, that you were a
devotee, fundamentally responsible for yourself in your
daily life and thus capable of considering the form of
relationship that is, bodily, the most intimate — the
marriage relationship. The marriage relationship has a
kind of seniority relative to all other relations, except
the one to the Spiritual Master, because of its uniquely
intimate character. Your spouse is the nearest "other"
in your life. Now it seems that we must drop back from
consideration of your relations with that first person
other than yourself in order to mull over the argument

of the Teaching, to discover whether you can be a devotee or not.

DEVOTEE: Yes.

DA FREE JOHN: Therefore, you still feel uncon-
verted.

DEVOTEE: I think basically that is true, but it is also
true that there is no doubt about my emotional involvement in this practice.

DA FREE JOHN: Well, what is lacking? Why do you
not love God? Why do you still worry about trying to
enjoy life? You must make your Way of life that of the
devotee, wherein you are fundamentally involved in
ecstatic Communion with God as a moment to moment
condition of existence. This Communion makes all of
your associations something other than they appear in
themselves. You need not live in the world concerned
about worldly things. You basically live instead in this
ecstatic Play, and thus your association with the things
of life is not binding, not obsessive, not problematic.
You do not require worldly association in itself to provide you with the fulfillment that only ecstatic Union
with God provides.

You must be emotionally converted to God, to
the disposition of Ecstasy as the very Condition of your
being, to a new response to the very Condition of your
existence, the very Fact of it. Now you are reflecting
the psychology of somebody who feels betrayed by his
very existence rather than someone who has simply

given up, surrendered emotionally and altogether to
God. You are worried about everything. You are trying
to survive and be successful in your life, in your practice, in your marriage. You are performing all the conventional self-protective rituals. Being a devotee is not
exactly what you are about.

86

However, it is exactly devotion that must become
the principle of your life. In every moment you must be
ecstatically surrendered to God, to the total Reality, to
the Living Being that is arising as everything and that
transcends everything, whatever everything is altogether. It is not a matter of knowing what It is. <u>That
It is</u> is perfectly obvious. Everything obviously exists.
There is a Great Process. There is no doubt about that.
You have not a fraction of wit sufficient to have created
yourself, as you now conceive of yourself. You did not
do that and you are not doing it. You did not bring
yourself to life. You cannot even make yourself continue to live. You have no control over anything. You
are not the knower in this affair, nor the Master of it.

You are totally dependent within this Great Affair, but you feel betrayed. Therefore, you are not in
love. You are not surrendered to what is your Master
and Source. Stop sulking. Abandon your infantile reaction, your sense of betrayal. Whatever you may think
created it in you, it is simply your own recoil, your own
vulnerability. On the basis of that recoil, you do not
love but instead mistrust everything and everyone and
defend yourself constantly. Ultimately you are simply
afraid and utterly without illumination.

Having considered all of this with me, what can
you possibly choose? Obviously the only desirable

choice is to love and surrender, but you must choose it from the heart and simply do it from now on. That is what it is to be manly, male or female. You are all tending to be weak, distracted, ambiguous. You are not strong enough in your character to give yourself to your own Source, to acknowledge That, to make peace with That, and to allow life to be Grace, to allow the Revelation of God.

Will you love the Source, the Condition, the Totality in which you are arising? Or will you turn away from That and be self-possessed? The difference is not a matter of belief. It is perfectly obvious that you are arising within a Great Process. Since that is so, what will you do? Surrender to it or withdraw from it? Either way will produce a totally unique adventure for you, and you must choose one or the other. The first thing you must do is to become self-critical enough to see that, in effect, you have already chosen the negative alternative. You have never yet consciously made a choice, but you have adapted reactively. Now realize that you must choose. You must now live consciously, one way or the other. What will you choose to do? That is the final consideration of *The Song of the Heart of God*.[1] That summary of the Way that I Teach, that "Gita," is the Revelation of God, but the response to the question, "What will you do?" is completely up to you. You can realize either destiny. The options have been made perfectly clear to you. Either destiny is possible in the physics of things. It is purely a matter of motion,

---

1. See *The Enlightenment of the Whole Body,* by Da Free John, pages 93–95.

either toward the separate self or toward God.

You can never truly be anyone's friend, or lover, or husband, or wife, or father or mother, or devotee, until you decide to surrender to God. Until that time, you are wandering in your attention and you cannot really be trusted. You cannot be faithful, you cannot make agreements, you cannot love, you cannot persist as love.

Truth is the great Realization of life. When you become truly sympathetic to it, nothing in your life can ever ultimately satisfy you. But now you are still involved in all the games of life. They fascinate you in one or another way, and you do not yet feel that you have found the Truth.

The Realization of Truth is an emotional matter, you see. The discovery is an emotional one, the change is an emotional one, the true practice is emotional. You are chronically involved in a process of emotional dissociation, emotional separation, self-isolation through the mechanism of feeling, which is the master or controller of the body. There is even a gland—the thymus gland in the chest — that is related to this feeling dimension. It is Life-negative by tendency. In other words, it is being suppressed, quite automatically, in people in general, because they are not exercising emotionally.

You are tending to be Life-negative as a matter of course. You think that you can be emotionally happy only when you are involved with relatively pleasurable things. No, having discovered this true emotion, you must practice it all the time—with a will, because you have no tendency to practice it at all! Rather, by tendency, you are completely wedded to this frightening, negative disposition. You are not surrendering emotionally to everything—that is, to God. To live in the disposition of surrender is just as logical as to live the way you do now. The difference is that the way you are now living is destroying you.

I, on the other hand, have no capacity except to embrace my heart's desire in every moment. Some people consider this self-indulgent, but to me it is obvious that one must always embrace the very thing one desires from the heart! Otherwise existence has no significance whatsoever and is completely untrue. That is why I am not inclined toward the program of seeking for God. One cannot approach God gradually or realize God eventually. The Realization of God does not depend upon any event in space-time, or in the body-mind. It could not be so. Thus, I have never been moved by any path of seeking for God. I have been moved by God to do all kinds of things. But in relation to this matter of God, it has been always instantly obvious to me that God is Present, Obvious, Infinite, Eternal, Absolute, Transcendental, All-Pervading Energy, the Self, the Truth of me and of everything. Even in consciousness, God is perfectly evident as all of That in every moment. God is my heart's desire.

Beyond Fear

90

DA FREE JOHN: You know how frightened you could become at this moment. A little uncovering of the unconscious would make you go bananas with fear. In fact, you would be adding fear to the experience, which would only be whatever it would be. But you absolutely do not want such an incident to take place. Yet you must become accustomed to passing through and beyond fear and death as a matter of course. You must release the heart from this stranglehold of fear, whereas in your conventional round of consolations you are keeping yourself out of touch with fear. Your consciousness is relatively superficial. It contacts experience and fear only superficially, but the emotional problem of your self-division is the root of all suffering and delusion. You are not relaxed at the heart. You are not relaxed altogether. You are not tuned in to the subtle force of the All-Pervading Life-Current.

You are uptight!

The more enemies, obligations, and worldly struggles you have, the less sensitive you are to the real Condition. The only ultimate, future, and sublime culture is one in which people may live with that deep sensitivity even in the midst of ordinary responsibilities. If you understand that this sensitivity is necessary, then you must simply practice it. You must provide yourself the occasion to practice and Realize this Disposition perfectly. You must manage your ordinary life responsibly, but simplify it. Eliminate its conflicts. Live serenely, but also with strength of will to practice effectively whenever you must encounter and overcome obstacles creatively. Practice this surrendered Disposition regularly in formal devotional exercises, both with others and by yourself. If, from time to time, you can also enter into a condition of total isolation within the spiritual community, that is also an excellent circumstance in which to practice. Whatever circumstances are possible for you, you must have the occasion in life to enter constantly into Communion with the Transcendental Being, and through that Communion to awaken to all the qualities of the Manifest Personality that is God.

You can practice this Communion only by transcending fear, by actual, literal, heartfelt surrender beyond all fear of death and madness into the Transcendental Reality. To do this you do not have to die or become mad, but your fear must be surrendered in love, in ecstasy. You must simply renounce your fear, give up the luxury of it, and presume surrender as your attitude under all conditions. When that attitude becomes true of you, you realize that fear is not inherent in the act and the moment of emotional surrender. Therefore, abide in surrender perfectly and you will not be involved with fear, madness, or death in the conventional forms that we fear and try to avoid.

Heartfelt release of fear is the secret of passing through the spiritual process without going mad. To the degree that you are full of fear, you limit your experience—and if experience is forced upon you, then you have no ability while fearful to view it sanely, to relax and surrender within it. You cannot surrender by relaxing and trying to feel better. You can surrender only by giving yourself up, relaxing your self-hold, surrendering your mind altogether to the Transcendental Consciousness in which it arises, and yielding your body to the All-Pervading Current of Life, of which it is but a temporary modification. You must surrender wholly and constantly to the Transcendental Being, not merely to its physical and mental forms of self-possession and separateness.

You are not very profound, you see, in your consciousness. You are basically fixed in your terrified conscious mind, providing no entrance into the play of life for what is superconscious and obstructing the illumination of what is subconscious and unconscious. You cannot view yourself directly because you are so afraid of the consequences of being yourself. Merely to be yourself is negative and hopeless, because everything you can see about yourself is dying in one way or another. You will find no peace until you have realized love, sacrifice, and self-surrender. You must surrender to God literally and release your fear. Such surrender is the foundation of religious life and spiritual practice.

Everyone who prepares to enter this Church is considering the emotional problem of fear and self-possession and all its qualities, mechanics, and effects. As that problem is overcome in Divine surrender, the fear that arises in every area of life becomes a matter of his (or her) responsibility. His wholeness and integrity must show itself before he is permitted to enter the Church. He must bring the fruits, the gifts, that are yielded in the fulfillment of this initial level of Enlightened or God-inspired practice. The most important gift the individual must bring, the essential sign that must be demonstrated, is a sane, whole personality, in a state of fundamental equanimity, founded in surrender of self and all fear to God, the All-Pervading Radiance and Consciousness. Only such a person provides a living foundation for higher practice of this Way, as I have described such practice to you. You cannot practice the higher and Transcendental dimensions of the Way in a superficial mental fashion. You must give up deeply, bodily. You must surrender physically, psychically, mentally, emotionally, and altogether. You must give up all fear. You must give yourself up in Ignorance to the very Condition in which we are appearing. You must have faith. You must trust the fundamental Situation in which we appear, exist for a time while always changing, and then inevitably die.

The Spirit

94

DA FREE JOHN: There is a body and there is a mind. There are physical sensations and there are thinking, visions, and dreams. Whatever complex of bodily and mental conditions is arising at this moment, do you not also feel the Spirit? Do you not also feel the Life-Principle that pervades all mental and physical states? Do you not also intuit the Presence of a Matrix within which everything is arising, the unobstructed, Infinite Form that is Absolute Radiance? You are aware of the Spirit in this moment, are you not? You know the physical, you know the mental, and you know what is felt and intuited to be pervading the body and mind. The Way that I Teach, the Way of real life or true religion and spirituality, is to breathe the Spirit, feel the Spirit, be surrendered into the Spirit-Force, and therefore always be in a disposition of equanimity, fullness, balance, and intensity, rather than your usual state of negativity, bewilderment, dryness, and mediocrity.

When will you be Spirit-baptized? When will you become submitted to the Spirit? Presently, you are fans of the spirit! You want to consider it, but you will not submit to it. Yet you know the difference between your present condition and the condition that you would enjoy if you would look, feel, act, and be completely happy.

The Spirit is not to be found in visions or in forms. The Spirit is not knowable or capable of being mentalized, grasped, or objectified. It is pervasive, flowing in everything, supporting everything. The Spirit is the

Presence in all, the Being of all, to which you must surrender with great emotion, with all emotion, with the entire being. The Spirit is the Vision of God, That in which all imagery, sensations, feeling, and forms are arising. The Spirit is omnipresent, presently Present. It infills everything; it saturates, supports, and moves everything. And we do not know anything about it! We are just watching everything arise. Everything is mysterious, moved by the omnipresent Spirit.

This is the Spirit's moment. <u>You</u> are not controlling this moment and you are afraid. Forget about that fear. Simply observe: Everything is being controlled! Everything is simply arising in the Spirit of God. You are not creating anything. Relax into the Spirit in this moment. Attain the equanimity of relaxing into the Life-Principle that moves all that is arising, and your life's adventure will change. Your life will be purified, and it will also be intensified. You will become Spirit-possessed, and true Spirit-possession manifests as equanimity, as resting in the Vision of God, which may be revealed in any number of ways.

DEVOTEE: It is obvious that I am not in control, that I have no idea of the overall pattern of arising. And yet, in a certain sense I do feel that I am in control when I suppress that recognition of the randomness of everything.

DA FREE JOHN: Everything is happening, so let it happen. Rest in the happening. Rest in the Law of the Spirit, the Force-Intention that is manifesting as you in this moment. You are trying to figure yourself out by

becoming less than what you are. Just relax into the
inevitableness of yourself, and you will see the Spirit
working, rather than a separate you that is somehow
independent from God. Although you seem to be in
control, your body is simply arising. The breathing and
the living of your body and all of its movements are just
happening. The mind that is going on and on and on is
just happening. Every process you can observe is occur-
ring spontaneously in this moment. No one is creating
anything and no one, no individual we can call by his
name, is in charge of what we observe. Well! Who is
doing it? Who or what is in charge in this moment?

"The Spirit" is a name for it, you see. To call it
the Spirit is appropriate because this name designates
the breath and emotion through which we recognize
the Spirit. Intuitively feel and breathe whatever it is that
we recognize to be generating this moment. Something
is making it happen. Somebody is breathing these
bodies, thinking these thoughts, moving this whole
world. All of this is somehow coordinated and interre-
lated as well. You are always trying independently to
know about the state of everything, but you must
recognize all forms of body and mind as pervaded and
resting within the Spirit or Radiant Being. When you
see this moment from the point of view of the Spirit,
then you will also enjoy the wisdom of this Vision. You
will see the body and mind, all the lower and higher
states of experience, from the point of view of the
Spirit. You will see the pattern of all phenomena
arising in the Spirit. And in your surrender into the
Spirit you will transcend all phenomena.

To surrender into the Spirit in every moment is to

96

Commune with the Transcendental Being. Thus, to "see" God is to enter into the disposition of surrender into the Living Being, the Infinite Radiance, wherein all events are always floating. First, find God. Recognize the moment. You may observe a range of physical conditions and a range of mental or psychic conditions, but whatever form your attention may take, there is always the sense that everything is simply arising, supported by what is Transcendental and All-Pervading.

To "see" the Spirit is to see the Vision of God. It is a whole bodily realization, like the realization that the body has at the level of touch. It is profound, psychic, prior to bodily and mental configurations. The total being of the body-mind touches the Infinite Being of the Spirit, surrenders into the Spirit with every breath, whole bodily, on the basis of true emotion, love-surrender. That surrender is the epitome and the practice of the Way of Truth.

The esoteric dimension of the Way of Divine Communion[1] is simply to breathe, surrendering with every breath into the Life-Principle with unobstructed, radiant feeling, rather than contracted feeling. You may surrender even to the point of suspension of the breath, thus enjoying simple establishment in the direct, intuitive realization of the Transcendental Being,

1. The Way of Divine Communion is the first stage of religious and spiritual practice in the whole Way of Divine Ignorance, or Radical Understanding. It marks the transition from commitment to the life of Narcissus, or self-possession, to commitment to the Way of Divine Ignorance, or radical surrender to Grace. The Way of Divine Communion is followed by three higher stages of practice: the Way of Relational Enquiry, the Way of Re-cognition, and the final, ultimate, God-Realizing stage, the Way of Radical Intuition.

which is the Matrix, Self, and Truth of every moment,
felt as the Spirit pervading all psycho-physical events.
In every moment, then, we notice the whole range of
psycho-physical phenomena or experience, and at the
same time we feel the Spirit-Presence that is making
everything happen, that is responsible for what is arising.

That feeling-intuition of the Divine Presence is the
aspect of this moment that is the Realization of God.
What is trying to become God, however, trying to
know about things, and trying to be happy, is the
"you" aspect, the ego-aspect of this moment. If you can
transcend the benighted exploitation of the "you" aspect of this moment and enter into sympathy with the
Spirit, the disposition in which all psycho-physical
phenomena are floating and arising, then you become
coincident with That in which the world inheres, and
you become Spirit-possessed rather than self-possessed.
Then all psycho-physical phenomena are re-cognized
by you in every moment, so that they become transparent to the Great Principle of the Spirit. Everything is
seen as a modification of the primal Radiance that is
Infinite.

The more profoundly you surrender wholly, emotionally, bodily into the Life-Principle, the more you
feel the depth of what exists as Nature and the material
universe and all the forms of experience, high and low.
Such wisdom relative to things hidden and unknown
arises when the Life-fullness, the Being, the Divine
Power, is permitted to show itself, to make revelations,
to infill the world and your body-mind so that you
recognize the body-mind in the Spirit. The body-mind

is not only what it seems to be in itself, associated with a pattern of experience. In every moment, the body-mind in its configuration of experience must be recognized in the Spirit, or Infinite Radiance of the Being.

Emotional conversion is whole bodily surrender into the Holy Spirit, the Transcendental Life-Principle that pervades all phenomena. Therefore, surrender to the Spirit. Become part of the breathing, rhythmic manifestation prior to mind, the Radiant Ignorance that is fulfilling itself in this moment as our own body-minds. Something is appearing as us right now. Someone is being us right now, and yet that One is not us. Do you know what I mean? That Someone is being us right now, that we are being dreamed by that One, and yet that that one is not any of us, is a Realization that you may imagine someone might have in the dream state.

We are all identities within the dream, and I am the persona in the dream who tells you that we are being dreamed, who tells you to notice that we are all simply happening and not creating ourselves. We can manipulate our future within that happening, but the happening itself is a mystery. We do not know what it <u>is</u>. We are not in the position of control. At the level of the mere existence of everything, we are utterly dependent upon the Spirit. We arise within the Spirit Being, Who is entirely Awake as this moment, Who is the consciousness and energy in which we are arising. That One is being all of us right now. Everything we seem to be is an expression of the qualities of that One. The more aligned we become to this understanding, the more spiritual we become, and the more wisdom we represent. This is the fundamental discovery, you see. No experience is senior to this realization. It is the Truth of experience.

100

Look. Something is going on here. Something is appearing as all of us. Something is being us right now. We—referring to ourselves in conventional fashion—are not in charge of it. We are just looking at it. Who is being all of us? The Spirit Personality is being this moment, is being these people, is being you. The same One is being you and all the people around you. The same Dreamer, the same Being, the same fundamental Identity, is looking at all others here. Behind the persona in this moment is the Dreamer, communicating the factuality of Himself and teaching the Way in which we recognize the Truth and become transfigured. The One of which I speak, the One to which I refer, the One with which I am identified, is All-Pervading, Transcendental. It is the Spirit Being in which we all inhere, presently. We all equally are identical to that One, and all of us represent, in some particular fashion, the direct agency of the one who is dreaming.

Consider the Spirit. Consider That in which the body-mind inheres, in which it is arising. Enter into such sympathy with the Spirit that any inspection from the point of view of the ego-contraction is transcended. Let it dissolve in the Spirit-position. You are all aware of the Spirit-Power-Being in the moment, are you not? That Being is God. You can create physical and mental reflections of That, but they never become more than that Infinite Substance and Mystery.

Somehow when we surrender completely into the Spirit, we all remember the Dreamer — and yet the dream goes on. We do not awaken as the Dreamer independent of this dream — for the time being, anyway. At the end of a lifetime there may be a period, like a period of waking up from a dream in bed, that is refreshment directly in the spiritual domain. In the meantime, however, and in every moment, you must live consciously in the Spirit.

We must all acknowledge that we are pervaded by and dependent upon the Spirit-Presence-Being that is felt to pervade everything and everyone. We must acknowledge that we are floating in the Spirit Who is at this moment sitting here with the eyes open, pumping the heart, being aware. What we call "me" is only a tension added to that One, something superimposed on what is simple and Divine and direct. "Me" is a presumption that is always talking to itself, while at the same time the Spirit-Being, the Divine Presence, thoroughly Enlightened, is sitting here as everyone! A conversation, our conversation, is also underway as a side-effect, a secondary expression of this Enlightened Personality. It appears to be a conversation about being disturbed, about being unable to integrate harmoniously with the Truth of this moment. But this apparent conversation is only the subjective murmurings of the Spirit, not its real existence. That existence or Truth is what we truly are.

The Vision of God

102

D A FREE JOHN: Have you forgotten the Eternal Vision? Is there something absent from your Enlightenment? People always want to know the path of life, starting from the bottom or lowest level. Why should you begin your consideration of spiritual practice by acknowledging that you are a vulgar, lower person, and that the way to Truth is going to be difficult for you because you are beginning at such a lowly place in the scale of spiritual growth? Why should you assume that there will be seven costly stages that will take you a long, long, long, long, long, long, long time to fulfill, and that you are probably too dull, self-possessed, and vulgar to fulfill that great path in any case?

Well, instead of beginning our consideration in this fashion, what if you come into the room and I ask you, "Do you see God? What is absent from your Enlightenment?" Then you do not have to answer me from the lowest disposition that you can possibly presume. You can just tell me or somehow demonstrate to me the point from which you begin the Way. I do not ask that you begin at the bottom of the scale of human possibilities. I only ask that you be as much as whatever is behind you. Right?

Well then—do you see God? What is absent from your Enlightenment? Is anybody going to answer my question seriously?

DEVOTEE: I think what is absent is the constant company of people who acknowledge and expect that disposition.

DA FREE JOHN: The absence of such company prevents you from seeing God and realizing total Enlightenment? Nonsense. That could not possibly be the answer. What is it then? Is your God-Vision being prevented? What could possibly prevent one from seeing God? Does God not want to be seen? Does God not want to be realized to be the Great God, Manifest, Unmanifest, All-Powerful, and Sublime? Could God possibly not be Blissful about the surrender of all beings to Itself? God would do anything to be seen, anything! Right? God must be of such a nature. God cannot be hiding. How could God possibly be hidden? By the very nature of the Divine, God can only be absolutely, perfectly obvious, not hidden, and never forgotten. What is all this nonsense about falling from God, then, or falling from the Vision of God? It is just propaganda! How could you possibly suffer such a fall —as if to have Realized God to begin with could ever involve the loss of that Realization!

How could God not be obvious in any circumstance? How could anything else be more obvious? What is more obvious than God in this room? Does anything else stand out so much that you cannot remember God? Is it God that stands out? You could enumerate endless qualities of this moment of experience, but none of them stands out as God stands out. You cannot lose the Vision of God. You cannot not have the Vision of God, and having the Vision of God, you cannot be other than Enlightened. The Vision of

God is exactly Enlightenment. Therefore, how can you not be seeing God?

Now you are about to feel guilty because you do not feel that your present seeing of God is a wonderful, ecstatic vision. Is that it? You are convincing yourself that you are not seeing God. You always act as if you are not seeing God. You feel that you are not seeing God, and yet God, being God, could only be obvious, is in fact what is obvious as everything and anything whatsoever! Can one do anything else besides have that Vision? God being God, God can only be what is obvious. Nothing outshines God. Even anything in its apparent obviousness is nothing but the obviousness of God.

Are you people capable of philosophy at all? Those who have seen God have the opportunity for wit and distraction, because they are only having the Vision of God. They are not serious anymore about the spiritual path that stands before the unenlightened. You are not other than enlightened. What could this manifestation possibly be but God? Without having to alter your perception, what could this possibly be but God? God is revealed not only in the fact that $E = mc^2$ and all matter is therefore equivalent to energy. God is more obvious than that. What could this arising experience possibly be? You can reach into all the ultimates beyond even light, but in whom does it all arise? It is not that this existence is a puzzle for you to ponder and know about until you Realize God. No. This is God. You can begin with and further develop negative interpretations of Man and the World, but the only obvious phenomenon is God. When whatever is arising is nothing but the Vision of God for you, then you are

free. Then all the propositions others make to move
toward their Enlightenment, Salvation, and ultimate
Realization will be nothing to you. You will be utterly
released from fear, self-possession, and attachment.

If you are seeing God, then see God. This is my
recommendation. What else could I possibly recom-
mend to you? You obviously do not have a problem. It
should not be so difficult, then, to begin to practice the
Way from the point of view of the seventh stage of life.
It should not take long at all, unless you continue to
forget the Vision and think that you do not have it. You
forget that you are seeing God even in those moments.
But once you realize that you are always seeing God and
could not possibly do otherwise, because there is only
God, then what kind of serious path of experience
would you like to create?

The Vision of God is not anything that cannot be
acknowledged. It is always acknowledged. It must be
acknowledged. How could it be otherwise? Do you
think the Living God is a demon who would insist that
you always blunder from the bottom of possibilities
toward the Great Reward? This path of experience
sounds like something that only you would require of
yourself. No Great God would ever require this of you!
It is just your own foolishness. Now that you have come
to me to discover the Way, I do not know what to tell
you, because I find that you see God and that there is
nothing absent from your enlightenment. You people
do not need a Way, you need a path! (Laughter) You
have already fulfilled the Way, and now you take up the
path of experiential growth. You are not on the path to
discover the Way. You have already fulfilled the Way,

106

and now you have plenty of opportunity to amuse yourself with the path. Not in lieu of Enlightenment—the path is part of what one does once Enlightened. This moment is nothing but perfect Enlightenment, absolute Existence. What is there to be unhappy about? Why should it be cause for unhappiness? It is the Vision of God, Whose changes are innumerable. Did you think you were seeing someone else? There is only that One. What is there to fear then? What can ever be lost? What can be gained at death?

Why should you settle for illusions, having come this far? You are going to die in any case. Why should you settle for lies? Why not be serious and really see and worship God? Be real, instead of seeking. Why should you spend your life seeking God? You should spend your life worshipping God. All propositions are nonsense other than the actual seeing and worshipping and Realization of and surrender to God. What else could life possibly realize? There is no path to God. God is only obvious.

Do you take what is before you to be God, or do you not? There are two ways you can live, based on either the affirmative or the negative response to that question. If all this is not God, you must proceed through a great adventure of experience, following many paths to the ultimate Unknown. If it is God, there is only one Way. What is it? To realize all this manifestation to be God is not to know what it is. It is to pass beyond the barrier of unenlightenment into God-Realization. It is to Realize That which is intuited in Divine Ignorance, released from the craving for knowledge. Is all that is before you God or is it not?

What do you say? What about the fear and sorrow you are always proclaiming?

DEVOTEE: They do not bother me.

DA FREE JOHN: You are inherently free of such emo-
tions? Then why are you not functioning like a saint in the face of life and death, free of life and death while witnessing them? Why do you have to pretend not to see God and to be withered by emotion and degraded by experience? Is experience anything but God?

SECOND DEVOTEE: No, it isn't, Master.

DA FREE JOHN: How could you not have the Vision of God then? Whatever this event is altogether is the Vision of God. If you recognize it as such, you allow it to be such, and you become perpetually established in the Vision of God.

SECOND DEVOTEE: Yes, that would seem to be the case, but I think our actions betray that Vision.

DA FREE JOHN: You do not live your daily life in the Vision of God, then, is that it?

SECOND DEVOTEE: That's true.

DA FREE JOHN: Why not?

SECOND DEVOTEE: I am just self-possessed.

DA FREE JOHN: You are looking at yourself and not seeing God? But what else is there to see? You are simply not convinced that you see God, is that it?

SECOND DEVOTEE: That is probably the truth of it.

DA FREE JOHN: You are not convinced? Or are you convinced?

SECOND DEVOTEE: At times I am.

DA FREE JOHN: Right. You do not yet continuously see God. That is your basic mood. Perhaps in some sense you are seeing God, but you are generally in the mood of someone who does not see God. Now you believe you must create some visionary experience to see God, instead of awakening to what is obvious. You think you must see something else. But what you have to see is God, not something "else." Else is else. This is God. If you recognize it as such, then you could not possibly be anything but Enlightened.

   Consider this: Must one have a vision to see God? Must one go through the seven stages of life before one gets to see God? No, one must simply see God in this moment. Restore your faith and be happy while alive. This is a much better choice than to choose to seek God. Until you begin to see God, everything appears to be both terrifying and wonderful. But when you are only seeing God—not some special perception or mystical vision—then you are free. Do you have to see something else, then, to be seeing God? If you see something else, it is still God. Then perhaps you can still see something else, too. That is why everything arises. There is always something arising in which to see God. The arising of the world is not merely a negative event resulting from past deeds. When you Awaken truly you see that everything, the entire universe, is the play of Enlightenment.

True Enlightenment is realized in self-surrender, release of your dissociative tendency in the face of everything arising. Thus, you restore your associative tendency with everything. All the monks and all the seekers want to simplify everything, shave their bodies, and renounce all association with the world. They want to dissociate in a manner that appears to lead to Divine Realization. Yet if God is Realized, if there is only God, then one's associative disposition, not one's tendency to dissociate, is enhanced. Presently you want to go within, but you must turn to Infinity. You want to go to One, but you must go to many. The One is already established. You think that if you find the One, all things will come to an end, but in Truth if you find the One, if you Realize God, everything truly begins. Instead of playing the world as if it were leading back to God, play it as God and as the work of God. How could it be anything else?

The Enlightened disposition is aligned with the associative tendency, the Radiant quality, not inversion or suffering. The native capacity of God is Radiant, All-Manifesting. This is God, not a place separated from God, not a moment away from God. Through our associativeness, our play, we incarnate the Divine — never finishing our play absolutely, for it never can be finished absolutely. Thus, we are always inhering in

God, functioning fully in our associative capacity while alive and remaining in God at death. In our Enlightenment we live eternally in God rather than living a lifetime as if dissociated from God and seeking to find happiness through the chaotic exploitation of experience.

110

Therefore, if you really are to begin this Way, you must begin it Enlightened, you must begin it in the Vision of God, you must begin it in the disposition of the seventh stage of life. You must magnify your creative and associative capacity. If you can be Enlightened, happy, literally free in the midst of all your actions, then that obviously is the Way, rather than any of the ways of retreat or dissociation, in which you fear to move, always afraid that you will die. Thus, there is only the Vision of God. In the Way, Enlightenment is the presumption of one's existence, not its goal. You must live presently from the point of view of the seventh stage of life. Truly that is the Way of Divine Communion, the Way of Divine Ignorance, the Way of Radical Intuition. That is the Way of which I have always spoken.

DEVOTEE: This disposition of total surrender is the one that characterized Swami Ramdas.[1]

1. Swami Ramdas (A.D. 1884-1963) was a saint of South India who practiced the "japa," or constant heartfelt repetition, of the Divine Name "Ram." He attained an extraordinary degree of mystical Communion with the Absolute solely through this method and the Grace of God.

DA FREE JOHN: That was his attitude. He saw that
everything is God, everything is the play of God, and
there is only God of which and as which to be conscious. Identify with the Self and surrender to everything as the Power of Life. Ramdas was smart. You all
can also enjoy that disposition. To be on the Way with
me would be sufficient. What else is there to realize?
The entire universe is literally God and God-playing,
as Ramdas said. The very One that is Absolute Unqualified Being and Consciousness is also the Matrix and
Substance of all manifestations, all designs. Recognize
the Divine as such, and nothing is terrible. To see God
is not to see something else. It is simply to see God. It is
to recognize this instant as God, as the Radiant Transcendental Being, and to be surrendered beyond fear,
beyond all the moods of self-possession and all self-
divided actions.

Why can you not realize the Vision? Why can you
not realize that the vision you are presently having is
the Vision of God? Is this not the Vision of God? Truly,
the entire universe is nothing but the manifest God.
Well, why can you not live in that Truth? Why can you
not simply live an Enlightened life as I propose it?
Presently you are struggling to prepare to begin the
Way. Unfortunately, you have become habituated to
exactly this position of always preparing but never actually taking up the Way. I am suggesting that you do
it entirely differently. Do you see that it is different to
persist in Radiant association with all beings and
phenomena while abiding in the Love-Vision of God

rather than to consider doing it at some point in the future?

Rather than seeing the world as a negative mystery, in which you must struggle to survive and know, you must see everything as the Vision of God, in which you are radiant, already happy, surrendered to God beyond fear. Then your role and the role of the pattern of arising itself is Transcendental and Radiant. The role you assume in the world is always healing, awakening, harmonizing, and thoroughly involved in the Transcendental Communion with God in every moment, the Bodhisattva's[2] role of always presuming Enlightenment. The true Bodhisattva's Enlightenment is not denied until all other beings are ready to become Enlightened. Rather it simply does not bring an end to the play of life or experience. It is simply a different disposition in the midst of experience altogether than that of the usual man, even the man of extraordinary experience. It is a way of always living in God through right vision, right understanding, right wisdom, right practice, and equanimity in association or relationship. It is to move beyond the disposition of contraction into the disposition of Radiance, relationship, founded in Transcendental Divine Communion. There is nothing to bring to an end or to destroy. There is no piece of the body to avoid. Live the body in God. Let it fulfill the

2. Traditionally an Enlightened being who chooses to remain active in the world in order to Enlighten all other beings. As you can see, Da Free John uses the term in a radical sense — the Bodhisattva's choice is determined by the Living Divine Spirit in whom he (or she) is utterly surrendered and absolutely, presently, and eternally Enlightened by Grace.

Law and be free and Radiant in God. Function creatively until you dissolve. Obviously that is what you
must be doing. The more profound this Vision the
more profound the blissfulness you enjoy.

Of course, you cannot practice the Way until you
represent at least the responsibility that coincides with
entrance into the fourth stage of life. Thus, the transition to the fourth stage is the real, true, and critical
point of Transcendental instruction for you all. Those
who would then live the Way must live it in equanimity, representing the human characteristics of one in the
fourth stage of life. You cannot be a disoriented or
disharmonious person, self-possessed and functioning
in chronic levels of negativity, bewilderment, and
frustration. You must represent the true devotee in the
fourth stage of life, because such a devotee enjoys the
constant Company of the Transcendental Personality in
all forms and as his or her very consciousness and being.

This manifestation that you see is God, the Self.
Therefore, do not divert your attention, do not become
absorbed in attention. Be relaxed, aware. Do not concentrate, do not move a muscle, do not turn anywhere.
Do not go within, do not go up. Do not turn attention
to the third eye or to the sex organs. Do not think. Do
not do any of these things. See that this is God. This is
the manifest Reality. This pattern is the Divine manifestation, as it is presently arising. What you see in this
moment is the Form of God. The configuration of every
moment is the Form of God. This Vision is the Realization of the devotee who is Awakened in the Way.

PART IV

The Truth of Our Existence Is Love

Essays

The true man or woman yields to the process of experience as to a lover. Such a one does not enter into the realms of experience in a defensive manner—cranky, rigid, full of self and knowledge. Rather, such a one enters into the present moment of experience as an act of love.

Experience, whether positive or negative, coincides with ecstasy in the case of devotees of the Real. They are sacrificed in any case, spoiled with wounds, and ultimately eaten by a mysterious lover.

Lovers do not fear dissolution. Therefore, they are active as submission, feeling, and ecstatic awe. Unlike the knower, who does not make love but at best presumes to love, the devotee of the Real is engaged in the process of ecstasy. The devotee exceeds all knowledge through love and ecstatic self-surrender. For such a one, knowledge is only a convention of ordinary order and thinking, whereas love is the method whereby the secret purposes of the universe are fulfilled.

Da Free John
Love of the Two-Armed Form

Only Life Overcomes Death

eath does not happen to Life. Only that which is merely touched and enlivened by Life can die (or seem to become Lifeless). But that which is Alive is deathless and never threatened. The being in Whom Man inheres <u>is</u> Life. And Life is only conserved and increased by the process of changes, or transformations. Life always persists, even after change and death.

Therefore, the idea that <u>we</u> are all going to die is simply false. It is a false, self-frustrating, and deluding presumption. "I" inheres in Life—and to believe otherwise is to embrace fear, separation, unlove, and all the philosophy that presumes death, rather than Life, to be the Principle of Existence. The idea that "I" can, will, or must die is a false belief, even a deadly act, founded on the failure to fully observe, consider, and understand our experience. When true understanding arises, there is only the natural and positive presumption of Life, which inherently transcends experience, change, and death through the Transfiguring and Transforming Power of Love-Surrender.

The Living Divine Being is not merely outside us and thus separate from our essential being. Nor is the Living Divine Being merely within us and thus separate from the body and the world. Rather, we <u>wholly</u> inhere in the Living Divine Being.

Therefore, the Way of Life is neither a matter of extroversion nor of introversion, but it is a matter of conversion, or self-transcending Love-Communion with the Infinitely Radiant and Eternally Living Divine Being. The Practice is feeling-surrender of body, mind, and attention — directly and via every kind of right or appropriate action — to the point or degree of Ecstasy, or Radiant Fullness of Life, beyond doubt and sorrow and fear.

118

Only Life overcomes death. Therefore, surrender to the Life-Principle and presume only Life to be our Situation.

Conversion

T he right motive of practice in the total Way of Divine Ignorance is not mere belief or any sophisticated strategy of self-manipulation. The right motive of all practice is the Revelation of the Living God. That is, each individual who is truly moved to take up this Way must have passed through a critical consideration of the total human situation as well as his own habits of action, feeling, reaction, and thinking.

Anyone who seriously considers the human situation will naturally observe that we have not brought ourselves into existence, nor can we continue to exist without accepting the relationship of dependence on various primal processes in the Realm of Nature. We are not self-contained beings. We are transcended by and dependent upon a Great Process, Reality, or God.

The usual individual, full of desire and fear, does not tend to consider this matter seriously in his moment to moment existence. He generally opens himself to random influences and seeks satisfaction in the conventional or popular stimulations of his body-mind. Thus, he does not truly discriminate between the influences that surround him, and he, therefore, does not tend to be responsible for his personal and relational existence — except for the casual maintenance of conventional patterns of behavior, reactivity, and popular belief.

But once an individual is awakened to the serious consideration of human existence, he begins to tran-

120

scend the stream of casual survival and self-indulgence. The source of this awakening to serious consideration and insight is always a form of <u>crisis</u>. That crisis may appear in the form of personal suffering, the observation of social chaos, and so forth. But it must always be followed by receptivity to the communication or argument of spiritual understanding, given through Divine Teachings, personal encounters with serious practitioners of a spiritual Way of life, and so forth.

Thus, the origins of the Way of Divine Communion are in the psycho-physical conversion of the individual to the Divine and Living Truth. That conversion is made through "hearing," or awakened insight. And it is a conversion <u>from</u> casual and random submission to the conventional stimulations of experience and <u>to</u> responsible surrender to the Reality or Transcendental Condition and Process in which we have found ourselves.

The conventional disposition of human individuals in this time and place is founded in self-indulgence and self-possessed struggles for experience and survival. The social machine as a whole is geared toward the accumulation of objective knowledge, or the attainment of the ultimate power to control and manipulate the Great Machine of Nature, including Man. It is this ideal and strategy, coupled with the personal habits of self-indulgence and separative self-interest, that is producing the drama of daily events or "News" that control and at times shock us all.

The individual, and the social order of mankind as a whole, must awaken from the chaos of efforts toward mere domination and exploitation of the World-

Machine. And, likewise, there must be an awakening from the disposition of self-possession, fear, self-indulgence, and separative or immoral reactivity (such as violent anger, sorrowful despair, lustful preoccupation, and so forth).

The truly human individual is one who has been converted from self-possession to self-transcendence, from self-indulgence to self-control and self-giving. The truly human society permits truly human acculturation, the development of intimate politics or human communities, and the tempering of all knowledge and technological as well as political power by the higher cultural ideals of the Realization of Wisdom and of the Divine Transformation of the world, of mankind, and of the human individual.

Thus, when the individual awakens to the Wisdom of true, right, and serious consideration of the human situation, he becomes converted to a new relationship to the Great Process in which we are all appearing. Instead of commitment to mere knowledge, power, and the ideal of exploitation or manipulation of the Realm of Nature, the awakened individual is committed to an intuitive and cooperative relationship to the Great Process and to the personal and relational or moral conditions of human existence. The awakened individual is intuitively established in a disposition that transcends knowledge about the phenomena of the Realm of Nature. He is established in the intuition of his actual and eternal situation, which is not that of ultimate knowledge and the power to survive by total and vulgar manipulation of self, others, and the world. The awakened individual intuits that his essential situation is one of Transcendental or Divine Ignorance: No matter how much experience or power he may acquire, no matter how much he may know <u>about</u> the conditions of Nature, he never at any time knows what any thing, or himself, or the world <u>is</u>. The world, and all phenomena, and even our own personal qualities always transcend our ability to be independently responsible for them. That is, we do not create the world, or ourselves. We are transcended. We depend on the Great Process. We do not now or ultimately know what any of it <u>is</u>. Existence itself always transcends our knowledge.

Therefore, the awakened individual is converted from experiential and social chaos, mere knowledge, and the destiny of self-possession. He does this by intuiting the right disposition of Man—the disposition of Divine Ignorance, or intuitive surrender of self into the Great Process or Reality in which the self is perceived or conceived.

The origins of the Way of Divine Ignorance are in this "hearing," this conversion <u>from</u> conventional or self-possessed knowledge and belief and <u>to</u> the intuited disposition of surrender or self-transcendence in Communion (rather than in struggle) with the Great and Divine Process in which Man and the total world are appearing, changing, and passing.

Thus, the foundation of every stage of the Way of Divine Ignorance is this conversion to surrender, or self-transcendence, in Communion with the All-Pervading, Living, and Transcendental Reality. The foundation of the Way of Divine Ignorance is psycho-physical conversion <u>from</u> self and self-possession <u>to</u> God and God-Communion. And the initial gesture of practice, founded on this conversion, is adaptation to new forms of action—that is, to right and self-transcending practices in the sphere of personal and relational (or moral) existence.

Devotees in the Way of Divine Ignorance are devotees of the Living God. That is, they live—based on intuitive understanding of the human situation—in an active disposition of self-control, self-giving, service, and spiritual or devotional surrender to the obvious Reality or Great Process in which we all exist.

Such devotees value their truly human intimacy with one another—and they also value the establishment of a general social order, or the culture of mankind, founded on higher Wisdom, restraint, and humanizing ideals. Such devotees also enjoy and value the esoteric or true spiritual relationship with the Spiritual Master, or the Divine Adept, who has become Full through the intuition and practice of Divine Wisdom.

What Is Wisdom?

Experience limits, defines, and compresses the being. Experience is a contraction of the body-mind. Experience is a limiting condition on the being. Experience is a contraction or suppression of the being. Therefore, all experience is a form of stress, or psycho-physical tension.

For this reason, the longer we live, or the more experience we accumulate, the more our behavior tends to become an effort to relieve ourselves of stressful tension. Therefore, the usual individual degenerates over time, because of the effects of stressful and self-indulgent habits that represent attempts to be relieved of stress.

But all our action to relieve stress in this realm of psycho-physical experience is nothing other than an effort to relieve ourselves of experience itself. We deceive ourselves if we presume that one or another complex condition is binding us with suppressive stress. All our experience is a binding or self-limiting force. This is not a merely negative fact. It is a presumption by which all wisdom is generated.

If we presume that particular experiences are the basic cause of stress, then our lives will become bound either to the suffering of those experiences or else to patterns of effort that are themselves stressful and degenerative but that seek release or escape from the conditions or experiences that we originally presumed to be the causes of our suffering. In either case, the body-mind is corrupted by the confrontation with stressful experiences.

Therefore, we must understand experience itself, or else we will never be truly free. And if we observe and understand experience, we see that stress, tension, the sense of suppression, or a limiting compressive force on the being is <u>always</u> an essential component of every moment of psycho-physical experience. There is no experience that can be attained that is inherently free of the limiting conditional force that we identify as painful stress. We may pursue and attain an experience that temporarily distracts us from some present condition of painful stress, but in another moment the very experience that was first felt as relief becomes a limitation.

What wisdom shines in this understanding? Simply this: The confrontation with experience is <u>inherently</u> binding, self-limiting, or stress-inducing, and this indicates that the process wherein we realize freedom is not in the realm or pursuit of experience itself but in the dimension of the transcendence of experience.

True wisdom implies a self-transcending participation in the conditions of experience. The native motive of self-transcendence is the law revealed to us by experience itself. Experience and knowledge are not the basic purpose of our existence. Rather, we are mysteriously involved in a process of conditional experience in which we are inherently and constantly obliged either to transcend ourselves or be corrupted and destroyed.

Those who will not establish themselves in the wisdom or true intelligence of the being are obliged to suffer their lifetime of experience, bound to the conditional self-limits of their circumstances, and otherwise

125

126

striving for release through desperate programs of degenerative self-indulgence and all the fitful politics whereby human beings seek to dominate and perfect their circumstances in the Realm of Nature. But if true wisdom awakens, then our commitment ceases to be directed merely to experience itself, but to the process of self-transcendence (or moment to moment liberation from experiential confinement) in the midst of the arising play of conditional experience.

Once we are awakened to the wisdom of a self-transcending or ecstatic practice in relationship to the process of experience, then we gradually cease to indulge the automaticities of stress, self-indulgence, and exaggerated efforts to know and to accomplish and to be overwhelmingly powerful in the world. We do not, however, turn upon ourselves and away from the relational patterns of experience. Rather, we simply <u>feel through and beyond</u> the stress of events—we recognize the component of self-binding contraction in every moment of experience and transcend that compressive force in direct relaxation of the patterns arising in the body-mind.

This wisdom is the intuitive essence of spiritual practice, which transcends all attachment to experiential conditions of body, emotion, mind, and psyche. The process in practice must be realized as a complete culture of existence, and that culture or Way of Life is learned by testing and instruction in the Company and the community of the Wise.

The Way That I Teach

The Way that I Teach is the Way of surrender, or spontaneous and total psycho-physical Transfiguration. It is the radical Way of native, whole bodily, moment to moment surrender to the Radiant Principle that pervades the body-mind and the total world. It is the Way of the transcendence of the egoic adventure of attention, or the self-contraction that is itself attention. It is the Way of surrender of the psycho-physical attention that is the ego, or the reactive self-contraction in every moment. It is the Transcendental Way of the tacit Realization of God, Who is the Primal Life-Radiance and Essential Being of all. It is the Way that is founded upon direct, moment to moment, intuitive, emotional, and even bodily Realization that the Infinitely Radiant Being is the Principle of existence, rather than "matter," or the contracted self, who is the disturbed, self-divided being that is always seeking its own fulfillment through experience and acquired knowledge.

Traditionally, spiritual life is viewed as a progressive path of experience, a progression of stages of the return of attention (which is ultimately the same as the ego-contraction) to the Source, Condition, and Environment of Happiness. The Great Path of Return, in either its Eastern or its Western mode, is typically the adventure of the contracted or mortally threatened ego's search for Happiness, for God, for Truth, the Answer, the Source, the Creator, the Self, the Ultimate Principle, the Wonderful Reality, the Eternal Pleasure, or Happiness itself.

The difference between the Great Path of experience, or self-fulfillment, and the Way that I Teach is the difference between attention, or egoic concentration in experience, and surrender, or self-transcendence in every moment of experience. The "Good News" of the Way that I Teach is that Truth is the all-pervading Foundation of experiential existence, and it is the Truth in this moment. Thus, in the case of the Way that I Teach, the individual lives on the basis of the always present surrender of the body-mind, or the state of experience and knowledge, into the always Present or Transcendental Life-Principle. The Way is founded on the Ecstatic or self-transcending Realization of God in every moment, rather than on the basis of the experiential dilemma and self-fulfilling motivations of the psycho-physical ego, which you usually consider to be the foundation of human existence and destiny. This Way of surrender, then, this Way of Divine Ignorance, or Radical Understanding, is the very Way of Life, which presupposes the Truth or self-transfiguring Happiness of God-Realization in every instant.

The Way that I Teach is not itself another path, separate from the progressive stages of human experience or growth and evolution. The Way that I Teach is the disposition of psycho-physical surrender to the Radiant Being, through which all inevitable experience may be transcended.

The Presumption of What Cannot Be Lost or Found

N o action or condition actually separates us from God — but the experience of actions and conditions tends to awaken the presumption of separation from God.

No action or condition actually brings us closer to God — but, once we suffer from the presumption of separation from God, the strategic manipulation of actions and conditions may tend to awaken the presumption of closeness to God or even identification with God.

In any case, God is always already, presently and priorly, the very Condition or Truth of our manifest existence. And it is not the presumption of separation, closeness, or identification relative to God that actually Realizes the Divine Condition or Truth of existence. It is only the unqualified, direct, or radical presumption of God that actually or inherently Realizes God—and that presumption is effective only in every moment wherein the experiential actions and conditions of existence are actually or effectively transcended in the ecstatic presumption of God.

This is the fundamental Understanding, the secret of Freedom, Happiness, Pleasure, Wonder, Surrender, Love, and Life — because God is the very Essence or Substance of Freedom, Happiness, Pleasure, Wonder, Surrender, Love, and Life. It is only when God, or the Reality of the Radiant Transcendental Being, cannot be denied or even conventionally affirmed but only tacitly presumed (because It is Obvious, no matter what is arising as experience) that the body-mind abides already or priorly Free in God-Communion. And only such tacit God-Communion, Realized moment to moment, provides the Creative basis for truly human growth, higher transformation, and ultimate transcendence.

We cannot cease to be Free. Nor can we acquire or attain Freedom. We cannot cease to be Happy. Nor can we acquire or attain Happiness. We cannot cease in our Pleasure. Nor can we acquire or attain Pleasure. We cannot cease to Wonder. Nor can we acquire or attain Wonder or That which is Wonderful. We cannot fail to be Surrendered. Nor can we attain to Surrender by any effort. We cannot cease to Love. Nor can we acquire or attain Love Itself. We cannot finally die. Nor can we acquire Eternal Life by means of the manipulation or effort of the self (or body-mind), since only surrender of self permits inherence in the Life-Principle. But Freedom, Happiness, Pleasure, Wonder, Surrender, Love, and Life are our inherent Condition. And Truth is the tacit presumption of Freedom, Happiness, Pleasure, Wonder, Surrender, Love and Life.

Idols

No thought or figure or any perception arising in the mind is, in itself, God. No thing, no body, no moment or place, in itself, is God. Rather, every moment, place, thing, body, or state of mind inheres in God. Whatever arises should be recognized in God, not idolized as God. Then all conditions become Reminders that draw us into the ecstatic presumption of the Mysterious Presence of the Living One.

The Transcendental Adept or true Spiritual Master is a Transparent Reminder of the Living One, a Guide to Ecstatic Remembrance of the One in Whom all conditions arise and change and pass away. Such an Adept is not to be made into the Idol of a Cult, as if God were exclusively contained in the objective person and subjective beliefs of a particular sect. Rather, right relationship to the Adept Spiritual Master takes the form of free ecstatic surrender to the Living Divine based on recognition of the Living One in the Revelation of Freedom, Happiness, Love, Wisdom, Help, and Radiant Power that Shines in the Company of the Adept. Right relationship to a true Spiritual Master is the most fundamental basis of the universal process that is true religion, and there is no basis for "religious differences" at the level of actual practice and Realization.

The Person of Love

The entire world, visible and invisible, gross and subtle, is the Body of God, and even one's own body inheres in That Body.

All that we can have in mind inheres in the Mind of God, and the very Being of God is That in which one's own essential being inheres.

No matter what one may do, there is no accumulation of changes in this world that would make a Paradise, since the possibilities of suffering and death would always be greater and more powerful than the summary of any moment's tentative pleasure.

No matter what one may come to experience and know about the internal and external domains of awareness, there is no possible accumulation of experience or knowledge that could exceed or overwhelm the Unanswerable Mystery of the Fact of Existence.

No matter how deeply one may enter into the Current of one's own inner being, there is no greater Bliss or Joy than the Ecstasy of surrender into the Radiant Transcendental Being or Person wherein the world, and the body, and all relations, and the mind, and the inner being are arising.

Whatever the world, or experience, or existence may <u>seem</u> to be, that seeming is merely a state or presumption that is determined and conditioned and limited by the body-mind.

However much of many, or other, or mine, or fear, or sorrow, or doubt, or anger, or desire, or separation of me appears—all of it is nothing more than an apparent condition of the body-mind in itself. But the body-mind is only a convention of experience, a temporary condition in space-time, whereas the body-mind and space-time always inhere in the Radiant Divine Being.

Therefore, we must not permit ourselves to be disheartened by the world, or by physical mortality, or by experience, or by knowledge, or by thought, or even by the emptiness of our internal seclusion. The total psycho-physical being must remain Awake in the Feeling-Remembrance of the Eternally Present Divine Being.

The emotion of the being is the Principle that makes a priesthood of mankind. The Radiance of the heart is the Means of a great and constant and ultimately perfect Sacrifice. The fire of constant Remembrance of the Living One, in Whom the world and the body-mind of every being inhere, provides the Altar of our Sacrifice. Surrender the world, the body, all conditions and relations, every experience, all thoughts and every part of the mind, and even the deep seclusion of the inner being into the Radiant Universal Transcendental Divine Being, the Only Existing One.

Such Remembrance, or Love-Sacrifice of the independence of all conditions of the being, is free of every trace of dilemma and self-bound strategy. There is no game in God, no awful demand for clever victory in the world or in the inward domain. The eyes may remain open, and the body may move about, but it is always a matter of simple, direct, ecstatic Love-Communion with the Blissful Person of Love, Who is Alive as the world, Active as the body, Conscious as the mind, and Existing as the inner being of every being.

The Song
of the Heart of God

The Song of the Heart of God
An epitome of the **Bhagavad Gita** *and*
the Way of Divine Ignorance,
freely rendered [1] *by Da Free John*

L isten to Me and hear Me. This is My Secret, the Supreme Word. I will tell you what will benefit you the most, because I love you. (18:64)

---

1. This essay is an example of Da Free John's translations, or free renderings, of the ancient Scriptures. Da Free John's own writings, his songs, and his talks with devotees resemble the radiant "gitas" and "gospels" of old, the sacred songs and summary utterances of Adepts who Realized the incomparable Truth and lived that Enjoyment among devotees. And his renderings of the Holy Books, like his original writings and talks, are the expression of the same living experience and Realization that were originally communicated in the sacred texts.

There is a tradition for such renderings or free translations. The medieval saint Jnaneshwar and the modern sage Sri Ramana Maharshi, among many others, thus rendered part or all of the *Bhagavad Gita*. Maharshi did the same with a number of other ancient and medieval spiritual texts. In this way living Adepts identify and regenerate the living Truth of the great traditions of esoteric practice.

Thus, Da Free John's renderings are a form of Divine Service to the vast traditions of which the *Bhagavad Gita* and the *Bhagavata Purana* are principal Scriptures, so that the ancient Way may truly speak to living beings. But Da Free John's restatements of the ancient Teachings are especially useful to those who "hear" and "see" him in Truth. For those who take up the Blissful Way of God in his Company, these renderings are Da Free John's own Confession of Love.

2. If you will surrender to Me, if you will become a sacrifice to Me, if you will constantly yield your attention to Me through love and service, then you will attain Me and come to Me. I promise you this, because I love you. (18:65)

3. Abandon the principle in all your concerns and all your strategies. Abandon every experience that may be attained as a result of desire and effort. Abandon your search for what may be gotten as a result of the various kinds of strategic action. Engage every action that is appropriate for one who loves Me, but simply perform every kind of action as a form of direct and present Communion with Me. Relax all of your anxiety. Be free of sorrow and fear. When you abide in Love-Communion with Me, the natural results of your various activities no longer have power to separate or distract you from Me. (18:66)

4. The soul that is born into the Realm of Nature, or the worlds of action and experience, advances from childhood to manhood, old age, and death, while identified with the same body-mind. Then the same soul attains another body-mind as a result. One who is truly intelligent is not troubled by all of that. (2:13)

5. All of that is simply the natural Play of Life, in which the two sides of every possibility come and go in cycles. Winter's cold alternates with summer's heat. Pain likewise follows every pleasure, since every appearance is followed by a disappearance. There is no permanent experience in the Realm of Nature. One who is truly perceptive simply allows all of this to be so,

and he does not add his own distress to this inevitable round. (2:14)

6. Realization of the Eternal Destiny is only possible when a man has ceased to defeat himself by reacting to the Play of Nature. Such a one is steadied by his own understanding, seeing that the cycle of changes, both positive and negative, is inevitable in the world of experience. (2:15)

7. Those who see the Truth of things acknowledge that what Exists Eternally never changes. And whatever does not Exist Eternally only changes. (2:16)

8. Such seers of Truth also Realize that the entire Realm of Change, even the body-mind, and even the soul itself, is Pervaded, each and all, by That which Exists Eternally. (2:17)

9. I am the Eternally Existing, All-Pervading, Transcendental Divine Person, the true Self of all. And My Power of Creation, whereby individual beings are made to live and change, is Eternally Active as the Universal, All-Pervading Life-Energy of Nature. (8:3)

10. I am the Divine Person, Who Pervades even the Realm of Nature, and within Whom every individual being is arising. I am Realized by self-transcending love, wherein every action is engaged as a form of direct and present Communion with Me. (8:22)

11. Men and women who are without faith in this Way of Communion with Me do not Realize Me. Therefore, they remain associated with the Changing Realm of

Nature, the round of psycho-physical experience, and the repetitive cycles of birth and change and death. (9:3)

12. Such fools already have Me in every human form, but they do not notice Me. They do not Realize Me in My Transcendental Nature, the Master of everything and the true Self of all manifest beings. (9:11)

13. But if anyone will live in Communion with Me, surrendering himself to Me in love, then even if his love is shown with nothing more than a leaf, or a flower, or a fruit, or water, I will always accept the gift, and Offer Myself in return. (9:26)

14. I am situated in the heart of all beings. (15:15)

15. The Divine Master of all beings is literally to be found at the heart, wherein the soul observes the changes of experience. Every experience rises and falls at the heart, spontaneously generated by Eternal Activity, the Universal Life-Energy, as if the soul were fastened helplessly to a perpetual motion machine. (18:61)

16. Therefore, do not surrender the heart to experience, as if you were in love with your own body-mind. Surrender the heart to Me, and to no other. I am the Divine Person, the Eternal Master, the Radiant One, Who Pervades the Machine of Nature as the Blissful Current of Life-Energy, and Who Transcends all experience as Infinite Consciousness, the true Self. If you will surrender your self-consciousness into My Tran-

scendental Consciousness, and if you will yield your experience into My All-Pervading Current of Life, then I will also become an Offering to you. You will be Given the Gift of Perfect Peace, and an Eternal Domain for your heart. (18:62)

138

17. Now I have Revealed My Mystery to you. Consider it fully, and then choose what you will do. (18:63)

Transfiguration

L et the heart speak the Wisdom of the Unity of body, mind, world, and God:

There is neither one God nor many Gods.
There is only God.
All the one and many Gods are Idols of the One that is God.

God is the Radiant Transcendental Life-Consciousness, in Whom all places and beings and ideas appear and disappear.
There is no God but God, Who is the Transcendental Consciousness and Eternal Energy that Radiates in Man and in the world of Man.
That One Pervades and Transcends the world and Man.
That One is my God and my Eternal Self.

Every possibility, whether full of pleasure or full of pain, arises in God.
Every experience is a spontaneous and temporary modification of the Radiant Transcendental Life-Consciousness.
If I surrender to experience, I merely enjoy and suffer, according to the mood and complexity of my various thoughts, desires, and acts.
If I seek within my body-mind for God, I am confronted and deluded by states of body and mind.
If I seek outside my body-mind for God, I am

confronted and confounded by the experience of all relations and events.

But if I surrender body and mind in the Radiant Transcendental Life-Consciousness, all experience Reveals the Living God.

God is not an Object of the mind or of bodily experience.

God is Transcendentally Present.

God is to be Realized as the Transcendental Subject or Eternal Self in Whom all knowledge and all experiences arise and dissolve.

Therefore, to Worship and to Realize God in Truth is to transcend the world and the body-mind of Man.

I am not separated from God.

Only my reflective and thinking mind seems to separate me from the Eternal Self or Transcendental Consciousness that is God.

I am not separated from God.

Only my reactive and loveless heart seems to separate me from the Divine Person, the Infinite Love-Radiance that is God.

I am not separated from God.

Only my bodily recoil from the universal demand of all relationships seems to separate me from the Eternal Domain, the All-Pervading Life-Power that is God.

I am not separated from God.

I must love, and trust, and surrender to the Infinite Consciousness that is beyond and prior to the world, the body, and the mind.

I must love, and trust, and surrender to the Eternal Life-Energy that is beyond and prior to the world, the body, and the mind.

God is the Living Truth.
God is the Way of Salvation.
God is the Eternal Master of Man.
By our acceptance of the Mastery of God, the Way of Salvation through God-Realization is Revealed.

Let the whole body pray in Truth:

I worship and bow down.
I surrender body and mind and all self-attention to the Living God,
Who is the Universal Life-Current and the Transcendental Self of all beings,
Who Radiates as Love in all directions,
Who is without center or circumference,
Who pervades and supports all the worlds,
Who consents to Awaken as Man by rising up in the lower roots of the body-mind, releasing all obstructions to the evolutionary Flow of Life,
Who Shines above the heads of those who are Awake, Transforming every part of them with Heart-Light,
Who is the Transcendental Heart, the Eternal Mystery, the Wonderful Truth, the Unyielding Paradox that finally Outshines the souls of all beings, every part of the body-mind of Man, and all the possible places in the worlds of experience.

Radiant God,
All-Pervading Current of Life,
Consciousness where I appear and disappear,
hear my breathing heart.

142

Awaken me,
to feel the Heart of Light and Love,
where this life and mind and body may dissolve.
I hold up my hands.

About The Johannine Daist Communion

The spiritual fellowship of practitioners of the Way Taught by Master Da Free John is called THE JOHANNINE DAIST COMMUNION. "Johannine" means "having the character of John," which means "one through whom God is Gracious." "Da" is a title of respect and an indication of spiritual stature and function, meaning "one who Gives or Transmits the Divine Influence and Awakening to living beings."

The Communion has three divisions:

THE LAUGHING MAN INSTITUTE, which is the public education division and the educational and cultural organization for beginning practitioners.

THE FREE COMMUNION CHURCH, which is the educational and cultural organization for maturing practitioners.

THE CRAZY WISDOM FELLOWSHIP, which consists of devotees who have Realized the ultimate stage of practice of the Way.

An Invitation

I f you would like to know more about the study and practice of the Spiritual Teaching of Master Da Free John or about how to begin to practice the Way, please write:

THE LAUGHING MAN INSTITUTE
750 Adrian Way
San Rafael, California 94903

The Books of Master Da Free John

SOURCE TEXTS

THE KNEE OF LISTENING
*The Early Life and Radical Spiritual Teachings of
Bubba [Da] Free John*
$8.95 paper

THE METHOD OF THE SIDDHAS
*Talks with Bubba [Da] Free John on the Spiritual Technique
of the Saviors of Mankind*
$8.95 paper

THE HYMN OF THE MASTER
*A Confessional Recitation on the Mystery of the Spiritual
Master based on the principal verses of the* Guru Gita *(freely
selected, rendered, and adapted)*
$6.95 paper

THE FOUR FUNDAMENTAL QUESTIONS
*Talks and essays about human experience and the actual
practice of an Enlightened Way of Life*
$1.95 paper

THE LIBERATOR (ELEUTHERIOS)
*A summation of the radical process of Enlightenment, or God-
Realization, taught by the "Western Adept," Master Da Free
John*
$12.95 cloth, $6.95 paper

THE ENLIGHTENMENT OF THE WHOLE BODY
*A Rational and New Prophetic Revelation of the Truth of
Religion, Esoteric Spirituality, and the Divine Destiny of Man*
$14.95 paper

THE TRANSMISSION OF DOUBT
*Talks and Essays on the Transcendence of Scientific Materialism
through Radical Understanding*
$10.95 paper

SCIENTIFIC PROOF OF THE EXISTENCE OF GOD
WILL SOON BE ANNOUNCED BY THE
WHITE HOUSE!
*Prophetic Wisdom about the Myths and Idols of mass culture
and popular religious cultism, the new priesthood of scientific
and political materialism, and the secrets of Enlightenment
hidden in the body of Man*
$12.95 paper

THE PARADOX OF INSTRUCTION
*An Introduction to the Esoteric Spiritual Teaching of Bubba
[Da] Free John*
$14.95 cloth

NIRVANASARA
*Radical Transcendentalism and the Introduction of
Advaitayana Buddhism*
$9.95 paper

INTRODUCTORY TEXTS

THE NEXT OPTION
*An Introduction to the Teaching of the Adept Da Free John
and The Johannine Daist Communion*
$5.00

INSPIRATIONAL AND DEVOTIONAL TEXTS

CRAZY DA MUST SING, INCLINED TO HIS
WEAKER SIDE
Confessional Poems of Liberation and Love
$6.95 paper

FOREHEAD, BREATH, AND SMILE
*An Anthology of Devotional Readings from the Spiritual
Teaching of Master Da Free John*
$20.95 cloth

REMEMBRANCE OF THE DIVINE NAMES OF DA
*One Hundred Eight Names of the Divine Reality and the
Radiant Adept Master Da Free John
by Georg and Pat Feuerstein*
$4.95 paper

GOD IS NOT A GENTLEMAN AND I AM THAT ONE
Ecstatic Talks on Conventional Foolishness versus the Crazy
Wisdom of God-Realization
$6.95 paper

MANUALS OF PRACTICE

THE FIRE GOSPEL
Essays and Talks on Spiritual Baptism
$8.95 paper

THE ADEPT
Selections from Talks and Essays by Da Free John on the
Nature and Function of the Enlightened Teacher
$4.95 paper

THE WAY THAT I TEACH
Talks on the Intuition of Eternal Life
$14.95 cloth, $9.95 paper

THE DREADED GOM–BOO, OR THE IMAGINARY
DISEASE THAT RELIGION SEEKS TO CURE
A Collection of Essays and Talks on the "Direct" Process of
Enlightenment Taught by Master Da Free John
$9.95 paper

BODILY WORSHIP OF THE LIVING GOD
The Esoteric Practice of Prayer Taught by Da Free John
$10.95 paper

"I" IS THE BODY OF LIFE
Talks and Essays on the Art and Science of Equanimity and
the Self-Transcending Process of Radical Understanding
$10.95 paper

THE BODILY LOCATION OF HAPPINESS
On the Incarnation of the Divine Person and the
Transmission of Love-Bliss
$8.95 paper

148

THE EATING GORILLA COMES IN PEACE (forthcoming)
*The Transcendental Principle of Life Applied to Diet and the
Regenerative Discipline of True Health*
$12.95 paper

LOVE OF THE TWO-ARMED FORM
*The Free and Regenerative Function of Sexuality in Ordinary
Life, and the Transcendence of Sexuality in True Religious or
Spiritual Practice*
$12.95 paper

PAMPHLETS

THE TRANSCENDENCE OF EGO AND EGOIC SOCIETY
$1.50 paper

**A CALL FOR THE RADICAL REFORMATION
OF CHRISTIANITY**
$2.00 paper

SPIRITUAL TRANSMISSION AND SELF-SURRENDER
$3.00 paper

SCIENCE, SACRED CULTURE, AND REALITY
$2.50 paper

FOR CHILDREN

WHAT TO REMEMBER TO BE HAPPY
A Spiritual Way of Life for Your First Fourteen Years or So
$3.95 paper

I AM HAPPINESS
*A Rendering for Children of the Spiritual Adventure of
Master Da Free John
Adapted by Daji Bodha and Lynne Closser from*
The Knee of Listening *by Da Free John*
$8.95 paper

PERIODICALS

CRAZY WISDOM
The Monthly Journal of The Johannine Daist Communion
12 copies $48.00

THE LAUGHING MAN
The Alternative to Scientific Materialism and Religious Provincialism
4 copies (quarterly) $14.00

CASSETTE TAPES

The recorded talks of Master Da Free John (each $9.95):

UNDERSTANDING

THE FOUNDATION AND THE SOURCE

THE YOGA OF CONSIDERATION AND THE WAY THAT I TEACH

THE BODILY LOCATION OF HAPPINESS

THE TRANSCENDENCE OF FAMILIARITY

A BIRTHDAY MESSAGE FROM JESUS AND ME

THE PRESUMPTION OF BEING

THE GOSPEL OF THE SIDDHAS

THE COSMIC MANDALA

THE ULTIMATE WISDOM OF THE PERFECT PRACTICE

PURIFY YOURSELF WITH HAPPINESS

THE ASANA OF SCIENCE

FREEDOM IS IN THE EXISTENCE PLACE

DEATH IS NOT YOUR CONCERN and THE RITUAL OF SORROW

WHAT IS THE CONSCIOUS PROCESS?

FEELING WITHOUT LIMITATION

CHILDREN MUST BE LIBERATED

THE BRIDGE TO GOD

TRANSFORMING SEX AND EVERYTHING and THE ADDICTION AFFLICTION

KEEP ATTENTION IN THE SACRIFICE

Other cassette tapes:

CRAZY DA MUST SING, INCLINED TO HIS WEAKER SIDE
Da Free John reads his Confessional Poems of Liberation and Love
$9.95 cassette

OF THIS I AM PERFECTLY CERTAIN
Ecstatic Readings by Da Free John
$9.95 cassette

DA BELLS
Tibetan "singing bowls" played by Da Free John
$9.95 cassette

HEAR MY BREATHING HEART
Songs of Invocation and Praise Inspired by the Teaching and Presence of Da Free John, by The First Amendment Choir
$9.95 Dolby stereo

TRUTH IS THE ONLY PROFOUND
Devotional readings from the Teaching of Da Free John set to a background of devotional music and songs
$9.95 cassette

THIS IS THE HEART'S CONFESSION
Devotional singing by students of the Way Taught by the Western Spiritual Adept, Da Free John
$9.95 cassette

THE HYMN OF THE MASTER
A confessional recitation of Da Free John's The Hymn of the Master *by a devotee*
$7.95 cassette

VIDEOTAPES

THE BODILY LOCATION OF HAPPINESS
A consideration by Da Free John
$108, 56 minutes, VHS format

THE FIRE MUST HAVE ITS WAY
A consideration by Da Free John
$108, 57 minutes, VHS format

Classic Spiritual Literature

THE SECRET GOSPEL
The Discovery and Interpretation of the Secret Gospel
According to Mark
by Morton Smith
$7.95 paper

LONG PILGRIMAGE
The Life and Teaching of The Shivapuri Baba
by John G. Bennett
$7.95 paper

THE DIVINE MADMAN
The Sublime Life and Songs of Drukpa Kunley
translated by Keith Dowman
$7.95 paper

THE YOGA OF LIGHT
The Classic Esoteric Handbook of Kundalini Yoga
by Hans-Ulrich Rieker,
translated by Elsy Becherer
$7.95 paper

A NEW APPROACH TO BUDDHISM
by Dhiravamsa
$3.95 paper

VEDANTA AND CHRISTIAN FAITH
by Bede Griffiths
$3.95 paper

FOUNDING THE LIFE DIVINE
by Morwenna Donnelly
$7.95 paper

BREATH, SLEEP, THE HEART, AND LIFE
The Revolutionary Health Yoga of Pundit Acharya
$7.95 paper

THE SPIRITUAL INSTRUCTIONS OF SAINT SERAPHIM
OF SAROV
edited and with an introduction by Da Free John
$3.95 paper

THE SONG OF THE SELF SUPREME
Aṣṭavākra Gītā
Preface by Da Free John
translated by Radhakamal Mukerjee
$9.95 paper

SELF–REALIZATION OF NOBLE WISDOM
The Lankavatara Sutra
*compiled by Dwight Goddard on the basis of D. T. Suzuki's
rendering from the Sanskrit and Chinese*
$7.95 paper

154

These books and tapes are available at fine bookstores or by
mail order from:

> **THE DAWN HORSE BOOK DEPOT**, Dept CD
> 750 Adrian Way
> San Rafael, CA 94903

Add $1.25 for the first book or tape and $.35 for each
additional book or tape. California residents add 6% sales tax.